Praise for Meeting God at the Back Door

Irving Moody's story was soul-stirring, bringing me to tears many times as I read about his life, his struggles, his insights, and his prison ministry efforts and successes. Romans 12:1,2 has taken on new meaning after reading how and why it impacted Irving's life so much. I look forward to sharing this book with others. — *Jan Bloom, author, editor and speaker; owner of Books Bloom*

Moody's story and testimony is nothing short of a miraculous and inspiring reminder of God's rescuing and redeeming His beloved children. I'm so touched by the story and will be highly recommending it to those in seasons of grief, in seasons of hopelessness, and to those without direction and vision. What a fresh taste of the power of the Gospel. — *Christa Hardin, MA, CLC. Author and founder and director of Reflections Counseling and Coaching Center*

Meeting God at the Back Door *is a powerful story of faith and overcoming life's obstacles. It's a beautifully written reminder of God's goodness that every Christian will enjoy. Encouraging, practical and inspiring, this excellent book will make you laugh and cry as you follow Pastor Moody growing up in the projects and persevering through all kinds of challenges.* — *Dr. Gary Cass, D.Min.*

This story of a young boy trying to fit in a world full of chaos will draw you right in. One of the lucky ones, he met God while in prison and is now a pastor and a prison ministry leader. At times funny and at times heart wrenching, this book is guaranteed not only to help the desperate and lost but also be entertaining and encouraging for all. —Dran Reese, president, The Salt & Light Council

Inspired and compelling! If you are struggling to create a new direction for your life, filled with purpose and promise, read this book and discover how to put God in charge and make him the CEO of your life. —Pat Wyman, best-selling author and founder, HowtoLearn.com

Irving Moody has poured out in gut-wrenching detail the story of his life and transformation. In real life, Moody is exceptionally put together and, at face value, you may not know the obstacles that he has overcome through his faith in God. The most difficult paths are reserved for God's strongest soldiers, and Moody is one of God's strongest.

After overcoming crushing poverty and the culture of violence that goes along with it, Brother Moody reveals in this book that putting your hand in the hand of the man from Galilee still supplies unquestionable strength.

This book will help many who are struggling with the question of why evil seems to triumph and have considered giving up. This book will let them know that God is still in control and that there is still reason to hope. —Sarad A. Davenport, M.Div. friend and seminary classmate

Irving Moody has written a moving redemption story. Pastor Moody didn't find truth the easy way. He tried every other possible option first: traveling from the projects of Virginia, through a life of rebellion, crime, drugs, jail and failed relationships; then to a successful marriage, family reconciliation, and ministry in Florida. Irving Moody has faced more trials and temptations than most of us.

His life is an inspiring testament to the transformational power of truth. I shed tears reading this book. I think you will too.—Trevor Loudon, author, filmmaker and public speaker

MEETING GOD
AT THE
BACK DOOR

From the Projects to the Pulpit

Irving Moody, M.Div.
with Maureen Guffanti

Meeting God at the Back Door
From the Projects to the Pulpit

ISBN   9781794489110

Library of Congress Control Number: 2019901835

To all of the many brothers and sisters who have been incarcerated: If anyone knows the power of being transformed and living a transformative lifestyle, it is you. To those of you who are still on the inside, never give up, never give in, and for the sake of God, never die to the truth, for the truth will set you free.

I beseech you therefore, brethren, by the mercies of God,
that you present your bodies a living sacrifice, holy,
acceptable to God, which is your reasonable service. And
be not conformed to this world: but be you transformed
by the renewing of your mind, that you may prove what
is that good,
and acceptable, and perfect, will of God.

—Romans 12:1-2 (AKJV)

(Author's Note: The apostle Paul was in jail
when he wrote this.)

Foreword

Time is a most unusual and unforgiving phenomenon of our existence. We often speak of time management but no one can manage time. We can only seek to manage ourselves within time. The only Master time bows to is the Creator of time, God. Our lives are a journey, a passage or process from one stage of life to the next through time. However, at some point, for each of us, time comes to an end.

My father would often say, "We have a long way to go and a short time to get there." "There" may be the fulfillment of our dreams, goals and purpose. However, we do not get to choose our starting point. We don't get to choose our families, our race, gender, and the socio-economic conditions we are born into; but into the world of unknowns and uncertainty, we are born. Many come into the world with little to be concerned about. Their families are financially stable; they may have a degree of privilege and security. No, their lives will not be perfect, but it seems like they came into life through the front door.

But for so many others, it feels like they came into life through the back door. It may leave them wondering what was wrong with them that this was to be their unfortunate existence. If there was a God and God has no favorites, then why do so many come into life only to find life is harsher for some than it is for others? Why does a wealthy nation seem to despise those who virtually built it? Where is the God of "One Nation Under God"?

Meeting God at the Back Door by Reverend Irving Moody is a must read for all those who may have felt distant from God while seeking to find a path through life and time. Those who have perhaps heard of this great God but believed they were abandoned orphans of His grace and power and left to find their own way.

For those who have had a more privileged start in life, this book is a great lens through which to see and realize that there is another reality. It is a reality that most will never see and, perhaps, have hidden their face from all of their lives.

Rev. Moody openly and transparently invites us into his reality, his journey in time, on his way to a glorious and intimate relationship with God. God was with him all along his journey, guarding, guiding, protecting and preparing. His path was filled with God's presence even when it seemed God was nowhere to be found. Through seasons of trouble, pain, ducking, dodging, fear and doubt, Rev. Moody, unlike so many others, refused to give up on life. When God was not on his mind, He was always in his heart.

While his path to God may not have been through gates made of gold in this life, he found the back door. God met him there and now he stands at the front door encouraging, teaching and leading so many others to come to the LORD who never left him. Those who have also had the "orphan of God" experience. And, those that the larger culture would gladly throw on the trash heap of life. Rev. Moody shows them the way to dignity, significance and hope though storms may rage and hope seems so far away.

It has been my joy to know him and walk with him on one leg of his journey. It has been, and continues to be, a great joy to watch how God has blessed, and is blessing, him with the love of a wonderful wife, a powerful and effective ministry and spiritual gifts to transform lives. Knowing him, walking with and admiring him continue to be such a blessing for me. I am convinced that reading this book will be a blessing to you.

Dr. Bruce Aaron Beard
Senior Pastor
Transformation Ministries International of Atlanta

Acknowledgments

I thank my Lord and Savior, Jesus Christ, for my personal relationship with Him and the journey that brought me to this place, especially writing this book, which was done only through His grace and mercy. I'm so thankful to God for sticking with me until I turned to meet Him.

My deep thanks to those who have helped me walk this part of my journey out to completion. First and foremost, my wife, Stephanie. My love for you will never end. You were the coals that kept the fire burning and would not let me overlook or give up on writing this book.

Next, thanks to Maureen Guffanti and her husband, Dr. Steve, who is always willing to help. Maureen, thank you for listening to my story word for word, for believing that there was truly a book inside me, and for shepherding this whole project.

To my pastor, Reverend Dr. Bruce Aaron Beard: Thank you for not just telling me but also for showing me what the joy of the Lord and being clothed in humility really look like. And for constantly and consistently demonstrating the unconditional love, mercy, and grace of God. Becoming a part of your fellowship has shown me what authentic leadership skills are all about. Thank you also to Rev. Beard's wife, the Reverend Gardenia Beard. You graciously shared your husband with me as he mentored me.

Thank you to my son, Rashaud. You inspire me. To my daughter, Vanisha: Know that I love you. To my brother and sisters: Your encouragement and support mean a lot to me.

To Miss Cherry: Thank you—you helped me at a time when my path wasn't clear; you were a bedrock for me.

Thank you to Pastor Craig King and his wife, Pastor Sandy King: For years, you both poured into my wife and me. Thank you for all the time you shared with us.

To Kenny, wherever you are, thank you for helping me believe that God had something great for me.

Thank you to the volunteers who have worked so faithfully with me in the jail ministry: Peter Bogacz, Damon Zuchelli, Vivian Roe, Mark Daniels and too many more to list here. The number of hours you put in with the inmates and the energy and love you poured into them has surely been an instrument of change in their lives.

Finally, a very special thanks to Sarad Davenport: Thank you for helping me envision this book. Your words of encouragement right from the beginning were an inspiration to me.

Introduction

The Word of God says there's power in our testimony, which is the public declaration of how life is different because of Jesus Christ. I know God wants me to share my testimony to encourage people—people that are incarcerated, people that are in recovery, people that are facing any kind of challenge or any kind of brokenness.

People like *you*, reading this book. I want to let you take a close look at how God can change a life, even in the worst of situations. I want you to know that there is no hopelessness in Christ, no matter who you are, no matter where you're from, and no matter what you've done.

It's very important to me as we walk through my story that I acknowledge the Word of God because my whole life is full of the Word. This Word is what changed me.

Part of my story is how the negativity that surrounded me every day in the projects kept me bound and trapped. I didn't know how to get out of poverty. My beliefs held me prisoner even before I went to prison. Even now I see guys I grew up with who still don't know there is more to life than the projects and the project mentality.

It wasn't until I went to prison that I began to see that education was a good vehicle to drive out of poverty, but that understanding came only because first someone introduced me to Christ. And it was only in prison that I felt a notion to see who Christ really is.

Who is He? And who was I?

Contents

1

Bruce, Gerald . . . and Kenny

"Son, I got some really bad news. Your brother is dead. Bruce was stabbed seventeen times. And they left him to die in the alley. My mom quietly sobbed and added, "There's more, too. Your baby brother Gerald is missing. Nobody's seen him. I don't know where he is. I'm worried to death. This is too much to take. It's . . . it's . . ."

My mom's crying was like blows hitting me deep, deeper than any other pain I could recall. She knew there wasn't anything I could do about this, either. I was in jail in Courtland, Virginia—not my first time in jail—and I was going to be there a long while.

After the phone call, I sat alone in my cell, feeling angry, feeling numb, and not knowing how to deal with my feelings. This news was bad, worse than anything I'd experienced.

When I got locked up, I knew that Gerald was in the streets too—he had pretty much followed my path. But my brother Bruce was always a victim; he never took the role of being the strong guy, the predator.

So, I put God to the test and that night in my cell I prayed. As I look back now, I know I prayed in a very strange way—I kind of dared God. I said, "If you *are* God, if you *are* real (not believing in my heart that He was), please watch over my baby brother, Gerald. I don't care how you do it; just let me know he's okay so I can let my mom know."

That was on Wednesday night. Friday morning when I woke up, my brother Gerald was sleeping on the floor in my cell, right at my feet. He had been brought to the same jail I was in, and due to overcrowding, had to sleep on the floor. Normally they don't put biological brothers together, but that night our same last name went unnoticed and he was put in my cell.

You might think that I would thank God and start believing in Him. Nope. Not me. I was anti-God and anti-religion. My heart was so hardened against God that even after this, when God came running after me in a powerful way, I still fought Him.

As soon as I could, I called my mom to let her know Gerald was with me in jail. The jail remained overcrowded. So, for several days, until the officers realized they had made a mistake, Gerald stayed in my cell.

Gerald had been caught boosting, stealing from a store to get money for drugs. Security had figured out that he and two guys with him were shoplifting, and alerted the police. The police chased their car and then chased Gerald on foot after he jumped out of the car when it stopped at an intersection. Gerald was caught. The car ended up crashing.

When I woke up that morning and found Gerald in my cell, he was what we call jonesing, reacting to not having his dope. I had heard he was using, or sniffing, heroin. People did everything in the projects, but his drug of choice was heroin. Now he was on the concrete floor, balled up in fetal position, shaking and moaning, the thin jail-issued blanket twisted around his body. Although Gerald was shivering, he was sweating. He hadn't been processed yet, so he was wearing his own shirt, wet with his sweat, and his eyes were watering. He looked a mess.

"Mo! Oh, my God! Mo!" I exclaimed. My family called him Gerald, his middle name. His first name was Maurice, so his friends called him Mo, or Reese—in the hood we shorten up everything.

At my voice my brother's eyes opened, then went wide as he focused on me. Neither of us believed what we were seeing. I helped him onto my bed. "C'mon, Mo. Get yourself up here." Once I got him covered with both our blankets I put in my order to the commissary for some chocolate candy for him. Meanwhile, I gave him some chocolate I had and got some from other inmates—Hershey's, Snickers, anything. Chocolate helps with the sickness, the DTs and the shakes.

Gerald went cold turkey in my cell. For days, he didn't even go out of the cell. His body went through the shivers and the runs while I kept giving him chopped chocolate from the canteen until he felt better.

Gerald knew Bruce had been killed, so we were both kind of grieving. We talked a lot about family, and what was going on. Gerald said he was kind of glad he'd gotten caught. Like most of us caught up in addiction, there's a part of us that wants to stop. But it's very difficult to quit. Being incarcerated is one of the best ways to kick it. You can't easily get drugs in jail. In big penitentiary facilities, drugs, alcohol and weed, all that stuff gets in. Some guards are in on it, and girlfriends or wives bring it in all kinds of ways—like in babies' Pampers. But in jail that doesn't happen.

It was good that we had each other then, but it was hard for me to be with him as well. He still looked up to me as his big brother, and as happy as I was to see him, I was sad because I felt like I was a bad example. In my inner man I was hurting. I had finally gotten past the tough guy thing, how I used to be in the streets, and I really was trying to get myself squared away.

"Look, man," I told Gerald, "When you get back out there, you need to get yourself squared away. You know what I'm saying? You're the baby—Mom needs you."

From that day forward I did everything to be the best example for him that I could be. I said to myself, "This will never happen again, ever. He won't ever come and see me locked up again." And that was my last time in jail.

When Gerald got out, he got back on the drugs, and, still following my example, ended up getting incarcerated several more times before he turned his life around.

The prison moved Gerald and shortly after that I was moved to a work release program.

Kenny

Even though work release was reserved for guys on good behavior there was still a lot of bad stuff going on. I just avoided all that so it didn't really bother me.

Funny—the one thing in work release that did bother me was this one guy, Kenny. He ran a devotional every morning, and a Bible study every evening. Everybody recognized his cell as being the church in our cellblock. He carried himself like the jail pastor, too; his voice was quiet and there was a peace and wisdom about him.

Every day Kenny would say to me, "God got something good for you; God got something big for you." I didn't want to hear it. I was raised in the hood, raised around violence, and used to taking what I wanted, so the idea of God caring about me went against everything that was my way of living. God's answering my prayer for Gerald I called coincidence.

My first response was to fight Kenny. I kept telling him, "If you don't stop saying these things, if you don't stop coming . . . I'm trying to give you an opportunity to just leave me alone. If you want to believe that stuff, that's fine, but don't say anything to me about it."

But he kept on saying it. Every time he saw me, he'd say, "God has something good for you. God has something great for you." It really irritated me, so one day I decided if he said it to me again, I was going to fight him. Sure enough, just like every other day he came down to my cell and said it: "You know, Brother, God got something big for you."

"That's it," I said, and I started strapping up, which is tightening up my boots, because we were going to fight.

Kenny was a stocky black guy. He wasn't muscular and he definitely was not a fighter. He was a little shorter than me, and older than me, by about ten years. I got my boots all strapped up and I was ready to punch him out. Kenny just stood facing me and didn't even flinch. He had no fear of me whatsoever.

I was used to guys who fought back, but Kenny had this calmness about him. Something in me just wouldn't let me hit him. I ended up walking away, while talking real bad to him, trying to get him to stop saying that stuff to me.

But Kenny never did stop. What happened was every evening around Bible study time, I found myself standing closer and closer to his group.

First, I hung out down the hall of our cellblock. Then I moved closer where I could hear what they were talking about. And before long I was standing right beside the group. I wasn't *in* the group, but I was standing right beside the group.

Mostly the group met inside Kenny's cell, and Kenny's cellmates were cool with that. Kenny sat on the floor. Some guys sat on the top and bottom bunk and more guys stood right at the door. They all would have their little coffees and cookies or whatever. Their behavior stood out. Instead of showing the anger and meanness you'd normally see in jail, they listened attentively, smiled and spoke encouragingly to each other, and prayed for each other.

When I was standing with the group by the door, what Kenny was saying was really starting to make a lot of sense to me. My thinking was starting to change.

How different these new thoughts were from when I'd come up in the projects.

2

Welcome to J-Dub

I was born in 1958 in Portsmouth, Virginia, a Navy town near Virginia Beach. We lived in a project, Jeffry Wilson Homes, or J-Dub. When the Vietnam War was going on, lots of folks called our project "Little Vietnam"—a war zone.

Sailors came to the projects with their pay, looking for drugs, women, or whatever, but instead found guys lying in wait for them. Armed robbery was common. Sometimes someone would get shot and killed for just a few dollars. It was nothing to be ducking and dodging every day, every time we heard a shot. First thing in the morning and all through the day and night we heard gunshots.

The only white people that came into the projects were insurance men. They would befriend our parents and collect money for the insurance premiums. Everyone knew they were walking around with a pocket full of money. During the time I came up, I saw two of them murdered . . . shot, killed, then robbed.

Our family moved into the project right after it opened. Our apartment looked just like everyone else's in the project, with an orangey-brown brick exterior and an overhang at the front door that made a small stoop, or porch. Our floors were concrete. Some people who could afford it added carpet; we eventually put in some sandy brown linoleum.

I remember my mom washing our clothes in the sink and hanging them on a line outside to dry. Then my uncle got us a washing machine. It was old and noisy, but my mom wasn't having to do the wash by hand. The washing machine went in the closet my mom used as a pantry. It was my job to clean out that pantry, and I hated it. I hated it because it was full of junk we didn't use. Sometimes I got rid of some of the stuff but then my mom would say, "Where's that—?

I'd say, "I threw that away when I cleaned out the pantry." And I would get beaten over that.

A lot of families in the project didn't have a matching kitchen table and chairs. My mom was proud of our set: a white Formica-topped kitchen table trimmed in red with metal legs, and metal chairs with a red pad on the seat and at the back.

It was noisy in the projects. When I started hanging out at around twelve years old, each group of kids or adults had a big portable radio playing music by groups like the Delfonics and the Jackson 5 and old favorites like The Dells. People kept their front door wide open, and music or TV noise would just pour out. During the week we always knew when it was six o'clock—every evening we would hear the opening music to reruns of the Perry

Mason show: "Daaa-da da! Daaa-da da! Da da da da da da da da dah-DAH!" No matter what house we were at, we heard it.

Graffiti was everywhere on the buildings in the project, done in all different colors of regular paint and spray paint. They weren't like the fancy graffiti you see today, with artistic lettering. Just stuff about people, like "Don't mess with this b----," things like, "this place is a hellhole," or "J-dub # 1," and all the awful cuss words you can imagine. I hated it.

People I hung around with did graffiti, especially behind the Center. The Center was the recreation building where we also had church on Sunday. It was big, square, with orange-ish brick just like the houses. Every Sunday the men in the church would fold up the ping-pong tables and put them on the side with the pool tables. They'd lay out twenty chairs on each side with an aisle between, and church was ready.

We had some characters in the project. We had Earnest. Ernest wasn't crazy-crazy, but he had some psychological issues, and he was handicapped in some way, so his movements were jerky. When I was twelve he was probably twenty-four. Everybody knew him, and nobody messed with him, because he was crazy, though guys would joke with him a lot. In response he would cuss them out. And if he went into one of his rages, somebody had to pull him off whoever was setting him off. He was a huge, strong man.

We had another guy we called Mr. Bob. He was an older guy, probably in his fifties. Bob always wore suit pants with a white shirt and a tie, and sometimes the suit jacket. He always dressed to give the gospel. He'd walk through the project with a megaphone, talking about the Bible and declaring Jesus was coming. He was like John the Baptist in the wilderness. "All this gambling, all this stuff, you'll never get to heaven that way," he'd tell us.

He came through the project every day with his little flyers, books, and pamphlets. He'd go around to people's houses. The old people would talk with him and he'd pray with them. Bob was about six feet three and a thick, solid guy. Nobody messed with him either. At one time he'd been in the penitentiary. I guess he gave his life to God there.

In the projects you had to prove yourself; either you took advantage of other people or they took advantage of you. There wasn't a middle ground. Either you were prey or you were a predator. It made for a very difficult upbringing because nobody really wants to be the bad guy, but to not be the bad guy was to be the victim.

Coming up, I decided to follow the guys that were the predators. I didn't want to be the bad guy, but even more I didn't want to be the one getting beat up. It was totally the wrong way of seeing life; but at that time, as I saw it, it was choosing one of two camps, and that's the camp I chose.

I didn't go to school a lot. My mom sent me to school every day, but I'd play hooky, and hang out on corners, shooting craps, doing things that weren't productive.

For me, school was not important; survival was more important. Being accepted by the project gang, by the older guys I grew up with, that was more important. Since

I had no father figure around for me, it was like the gang became my father. I looked up to them and wanted to prove myself to them.

Looking to Impress the Street

I looked to the streets for gratification. I was looking to impress the street. I wanted to be known as a tough guy, someone who could handle himself.

Trouble . . . it was waiting to put its arms around me. All the trouble you could ever want was right there for you. I walked into trouble wholeheartedly. I was excited about learning how to smoke weed, play dice, and mess around with guns. That was all part of what the projects were to me.

As I look back, I see that I just wanted to be loved. I know my mom loved me, but she was raising seven kids by herself. And she had to work. It wasn't until much later that I saw how what I was doing affected my family.

3

My Family

There wasn't a father in our home because my father was incarcerated. Even when I was a little kid, my dad was already going in and out of jail. The first time I saw him was in the penitentiary. Sometimes, when he got out, he would come by.

His name was Irving, so I'm a junior. He was five feet nine inches, and fit, but he wasn't muscular. His hair was cut short, a military-style box cut. He was dark-skinned, and had high cheekbones. I look like him.

My dad could draw and write. He was a strong narrator. I've written a lot of poems and stories, so I got that talent from him. One of my sisters and a half-brother got our dad's artistic ability. His art talent was unbelievable. He could walk into a room and look around for about fifteen minutes. Then he could go into another room and perfectly sketch everything he'd seen. My dad was an exceptional artist.

He was also a forger. That's how he ended up in prison.

When I visited my dad in the penitentiary he would tell me, "You don't want to come here, you don't want to get locked up. You're caged like an animal. You can't do nothing; you got to follow the regulations."

But it was like a badge of honor to us in the hood to get locked up. That meant you passed the hood test.

My thought about my dad being in the penitentiary was, "I'm just like him. He's in jail; the same thing's going to happen to me. I just kind of lived knowing I was going to be locked up. I almost looked forward to it happening. The way I saw it was "all black men get locked up 'cuz they're against us. Sooner or later they're going to catch up with us. So, do what you gotta do, 'cuz it's comin'. You can't get away from it."

My Mom

My mom was not a big woman, being about five feet six inches tall, and slim, back then. She never drove a car. She walked and rode the bus, to work, back, everywhere. She walked a lot and she worked hard, so she had strong legs . . . and strong arms. She had a good disposition, smiled often, and she could joke and laugh easily. She could get real angry too.

I remember when I was about eight years old, I asked my mom for money to buy a spinning top because all my friends had one. They cost a quarter at the local store, The Grill. She wouldn't give me the money.

So I went into her pocketbook and took what I thought was a dollar bill, but it was a ten. I went across the street to The Grill. That store sold everything; food, toys, toiletries, laundry detergent—even cooked food, like sausage and rice, from the kitchen they had set up there.

I bought a green spinning top, and went back to our place. Even as I was putting all that change into her purse, I knew I was going to get it. But I didn't have sense enough to return the top and ask for my money back. I went out to play with my spinning top.

When I came home I walked into our living room and my mom was standing there, waiting. She said, "Where is it? Where is that spinning top? 'Cuz I know you bought it 'cuz you ain't have sense enough. You took my ten-dollar bill and put the change back. Nobody did it but you. Don't even start lyin', cuz if you lie . . ." and I just started crying. She was fireball mad.

I knew, I knew, what was coming.

She aimed for my head with a frying pan, her big old Teflon skillet she used to cook everything. But I put my arms up, and the frying pan felt like it broke my wrist. She hit me again, caught the back of my head. But she wasn't done. That was just the first thing, because that's what she got her hands on. She said, "Get in the room 'cuz you're gettin' it."

She came into my room carrying the broom. I tried to block it and got knots in my arms from the stick. She turned the broom around, her blows punctuating her words: " Any time I tell you *no*, it's NO! And don't' you EVER steal from me . . .!"

I got one of my worst beatings that day. She beat me so hard I had to pick pieces of straw out of the skin on my arms. She beat the bricks off me. But I knew I had done wrong. I had to own up to that. I had put stuff off on my brothers and sisters before, but she knew it was me who had stolen from her. And she was very, very angry.

It wasn't the first time I stole from her.

It was the first time she caught me.

I stayed in my room the rest of the night and cried. I got up a couple times and she said, "What're you doin' up?"

"My arms are hurtin'. They're sore."

"Let me see 'em." She took a look, and called to my sister, Angie. "Go put some alcohol on his arms."

That was just one time in a long line of my being stupid and rebellious.

Back then my mom worked as a housekeeper and nanny for a family, but as I got a few years older she got a job in housekeeping at the hospital and worked nights. She'd make sure everybody was in the house, then she'd put on her uniform, a white dress and white shoes, and go to her job. We'd go to bed, and when we woke up, she'd be home.

As I began to get in the streets, it was the *perfect* setup for me. I'd wait for her to leave, and I'd hit the streets until midnight or one or two in the morning. There's nothing out there but trouble that time of night. Most of the guys that were making trouble were older, and they took me under their wing.

I remember one night my mom went to work—and I snuck out. But for some reason she came back home. I don't know why; maybe she was sick. It was around one o'clock in the morning. Normally I went out my window, leaving it unlocked. I didn't want my sisters and brothers to know because when my mom left she'd tell us, "Don't let anybody in the house."

On this night, I came back to the house and the window was locked. I knocked on the window, calling my sister, not knowing that my mom had come back home and she was waiting for me. My mom told my sister to tell me to go to the back door and then she placed herself behind the door. And she had the broom.

I knocked on the door, and finally it opened and I was looking at my sister. She unlocked the screen door. I walked in and my mom stepped out from behind the door . . .

She just *cracked* me. Ohhh! It felt like one of those cartoons where you see the little birds flying around a person's head. I wasn't knocked out, but I was certainly dazed . . . dazed and dizzy.

I felt my way past the sink and the stove, just trying to make it to my bedroom because I didn't want to get hit again. I fell in bed. Man, she hit me so hard my head was spinning. I could hear my mom tell my sister, "Go in there and make sure he all right. I really didn't mean to hit him that hard."

The next day my mom scolded me, as she always did: "I told you, don't be leaving out of this house when I'm gone. Anything can happen out there. Those streets are bad."

But I went right back out the window the next night.

Excepting my rebellion, we all pretty much did what my mom said—especially after we got a beating. My sisters got the strap more than anything else. For me, besides that frying pan and the broom, many times I'd catch her shoe—anything she could get her hands on; it was always kind of spontaneous.

If my mom hit you, you had really been hit. She was heavy-handed. That's what we called it back then. She never punched me, but she would smack me, especially in the back of the head. She would smack the dickens out of us. And the bad part was we never saw it coming. She would come in and . . . Whap! "I told you!"

Today this could be called child abuse. It wasn't. Back then that was just the way our parents carried. You did what was right or you got your butt tore up.

Any night I got a beating, I was so sore it was hard to sleep. But I knew I deserved every bit of it. I was really an outrageously rebellious child.

When I look back now I realize how much she loved us and how much we made life a hell for her. My mom didn't see me become a pastor, but she saw me straighten out. Her last year she knew I was a different son.

My Siblings

With my dad, who was her only husband, my mom had three kids. I'm the third child, and the first son. My sister Angie is two years older and my sister Alice, who was named after my mom, was one year older than me. Angie was like a second mom to me. She was a rule-follower and kind of innocent, or green. I never wanted her to know what I was doing. Angie moved to Boston, got married, and she and her husband have stayed married to this day. Alice, or Peaches as we called her, died in 2015 from a lifetime of drugs and alcohol. We were comforted, however, in knowing she had accepted Christ.

My mom's first boyfriend, Bruce, fathered two children with her: Bruce, about two years younger than me; and Amanda, born one year later. Amanda escaped the cycle of the projects because she ended up living with my great-aunt and great-uncle out in the suburbs. They tried to get each of us to stay with them, but for me it felt like they were trying to take me from my other family, the gang, and I refused to leave the project.

One year after Amanda was born, my mom and her next boyfriend, Big Bud, had a girl, Jacqueline, my youngest sister, who we called Gigi. Gigi took care of my mom when she was sick and cared for her until she passed, when Gigi was in her late thirties. It's almost like Gigi stopped living her own life. The rest of us had been moving out but she didn't leave. Gigi eventually got married but never had any kids. Gigi has a caring personality, very loving.

My youngest brother, Gerald, was born two years after Gigi. When he was grown-up he was heavier than me, though I was taller. He had a thick neck and arms. People would say, "Why are you calling him your *little* brother? He's your *big* brother."

People have asked me about my stepdads. I never thought of them that way; my mom never married them. Her boyfriend Bruce was only at our house on weekends.

Big Bud was the last man in my mom's life. He was a big dude. I'm not even sure what his real name was—everyone just called him Big Bud. He was a long-distance truck driver. The only time he would come to our house was around one of his driving jobs. After he left his home or before he went home after a trip, he spent a day or two over at our house.

I knew where Big Bud lived. I knew his whole family; he was married and had other kids. I went to school with his daughter Deborah. Deborah and her brother were close to my age. We knew of each other, but we kind of acted like we didn't know. We kept our distance. We didn't disrespect each other and we never talked about our parents with each other.

It was crazy because everybody in J-Dub knew. And stuff like this had gone on for generations. My grandmother knew her husband had other women in other parts of town and they knew about grandma and the family he had.

I was in my thirties when I learned that after my dad got out of prison he went to New Jersey and had a whole other family, then left them too. My half-sister is a model and my half-brother is incarcerated.

Bruce and Gerald — Following Their Big Brother

My brother Bruce was a chronic asthmatic; he was about three inches shorter than the rest of us, thin, and always frail and sickly, with beady kind of eyes. He wheezed in and out when he breathed, and always looked like he had a cold. He had a little thing that he squirted in his nose once in a while to help him breathe, but it didn't seem to change anything. His nickname was Peanut, or Nut.

Bruce wore my hand-me downs. He was so bony they kind of hung loose on him. And except for once, when he grew it out, he always had a TWA—that stands for teeny-weeny Afro.

My mom made me watch out for him so he was always tagging along. I hated that because I was hanging out with guys who were shooting craps and stealing from the store. I never wanted him doing what I was doing.

If we were in the park, Bruce would find somebody else to play with. "Stay right here," I'd say to him. And he'd stay there, most always. Once in a while I'd have to go find him. There were a couple times I went home without him, and my mom said, "Where is he? Where is Peanut?"

When I told her that I had looked around and he was gone, I got a whipping and had to go out and find him.

It wasn't like he had any mental condition; though sickly, mentally he was fine. The way he fit in is he became really good at telling jokes, and everybody came to know him as this funny guy that cracked jokes.

Back in the hood we joked on each other. You didn't want to get in a sparring match with guys who could really joke because they were going to embarrass you. Peanut was one of those guys. One time he was joking with one of my friends, a guy my age, and I warned my friend not to joke with Bruce. But they got into it anyway.

My friend had a tooth that stuck way out. Peanut said to him, "I know you ain't talkin', I *know* you ain't talkin'; because this is how you look when you talk." And Peanut put his hand by his mouth with his finger stuck straight out, wiggling.

Everybody cracked up. My friend was embarrassed but he was good, he was cool. Sometimes people got mad when they got embarrassed and it ended up in some real serious fights. With Peanut nobody retaliated because they knew he was sickly. So they would just say, "Good joke, Man, you got me."

I did have to protect Peanut sometimes. Once a guy started messing with Peanut. I was a ways over with my crowd, and I saw it happening, so I ran over there. By the time I got there, this kid had pushed Peanut a couple times, and knocked him down. I smashed the guy, and told him, "This is my brother. This is not anybody for you to mess with. If I *ever* see you touch him again I will kick your . . ." I used some words that are not really fitting to repeat.

He got the message loud and clear.

Peanut started drinking as a teenager. I think that's another way he was just trying to fit in. He wasn't strong, he wasn't tough, and he had a big brother that had a reputation, so everybody talked about me and not him.

Peanut's jokes gave him an identity, but he was even funnier when he was drunk. During those times they called him Wino, because all he drank was wine. Wine became his addiction.

Bruce did go to school more than me. But he didn't finish school either. That wine became his way of living. Later on, he started to be the project handyman, helping old ladies, running errands, and cutting grass. They knew Peanut. He had his own little clientele.

But when he was a teenager, late at night when the real stuff started Bruce would be in the house. Most good kids were in the house by nine o' clock. Gerald, on the other hand, at some point learned how I moved and would come out at night, too. He was carrying on the Moody name in the projects. Most of the crew Gerald hung out with were the younger brothers or cousins of the crew I hung out with, and they were doing the same things we were doing; stealing, fighting, going to different projects, being tough guys.

When I first found out Gerald, at fifteen, was drinking beer and smoking weed, it bothered me.

We may have been teenagers, but it was easy for us to get alcohol.

MEETING GOD AT THE BACK DOOR

4

The Bootlegger and the Church

We had a guy in J-Dub selling liquor out of his home, Boss, the bootlegger. Every day my brother Bruce was in that bootlegger house, several times a day, and so was I. We'd walk in his front door, through the living room, and into the kitchen where the liquor was sold. The refrigerator was filled with cans and bottles of beer, bottles of gin, and bottles of white wine. Next to the refrigerator Styrofoam cups and shot glasses were stacked. Everything was sold by the cup or glass. A shot of wine in a Styrofoam cup cost two dollars. A shot glass of liquor was one dollar.

We'd buy it there and mostly drink it right there or outside the kitchen door in the backyard. It's like a bar, only all day and all night. Every week the bootlegger stocked up. Boss is not even ten years older than me, but he's been selling liquor from his house as long as I can remember. He made over five hundred dollars a day selling those two-dollar and one-dollar drinks. And that's still going on now. In 2008, calling it a high-crime area, the city razed J-Dub. In its place the city built single-family homes and apartments. Boss just reopened shop in another house nearby.

The Church

We were sent to church every week. My mom stayed home, catching up on sleep, cooking and cleaning, even though the pastor, Malachi, and his wife, Alice, were her uncle and aunt. They both were short and plump; she fed him well, Virginia hams and all that good stuff. They were a model family—they went to church every Sunday, came home, had dinner, and then went back to church.

The pastor and his wife talked about God a lot, but I was dodging bullets day and night. I saw people getting shot, beat up and doing drugs out in the open. I saw all this wrong, and since God was supposed to be right, I thought, "Where is He? He must not know about the projects. Or He doesn't care."

Though I didn't want to go, every Sunday morning I was forced to dress in nice clothes and head down to the church. At our house we had what we called "old timey clothes" to wear to church. Dresses for the girls and khakis and plaid shirts for us boys. My uncle at the church passed on to us used clothing that was given to his church. All of my sisters hated their Sunday clothes, and hated people seeing them with their dresses on. Our mom would fix their hair Saturday night and put a bow in it Sunday morning. When mini-skirts came into style, my sisters had a couple our stylish cousin in Boston sent them. They'd wear those to parties in the project. But to church they would wear skirts and dresses that came right above the knee. Nothing shorter.

If you wore something higher than that, you were tagged by the parents as "a ho." If my mom saw a girl in a short skirt, she'd mutter about the girl's mom, "I don't know why she let her come out like that."

The only time we got new clothes was for Easter. You had to be dressed up for Easter. I would wear a suit with a tie; and the girls wore brand new dresses, with brand new shoes and stockings. Easter was big in the projects, big in the African-American community. It was bigger than Christmas. You might not get anything for Christmas, but you always got a new outfit for Easter.

I would wear my new suit for Easter and then never wear it again. My mom would try to make me wear it, but when I was young I would cry and ask her why I had to wear it. When I was older I sometimes put on the white shirt, tie and pants knowing I wasn't going to be going to church anyway.

My sisters and I and my younger brothers all started out together for church. We would head down to the main street through the middle of the project towards the Center. Sometimes the older kids in the project would pick on me, saying, "Look at him with his Sunday suit on. Look at that little nigger. Who does he think he is?" I didn't care how big they were; if I had to, I'd fight them. Nobody was going to punk me!

As I grew older, once I left the house I would roll up my sleeves, take off my tie, and pull my shirt out and let it hang. My mom could get me to leave the house in my Sunday suit until I was about thirteen. Then I wore jeans. I told her, "A lot of kids wear jeans. It's okay to wear jeans to church."

I didn't want to sit in Sunday school class. I didn't want to sing Sunday school songs, and I didn't want to be in Vacation Bible School in the summer. I preferred to shoot dice behind the Center with my friends. I often did.

Behind the Center was one of the places where you weren't out in the open on the main drag. So, everybody met behind the center, especially everybody that was doing wrong.

Even though they knew I was living the project life, doing wrong, my uncle and aunt were always loving, inviting me to church, encouraging me to do the right thing. It seemed like every time they saw me they said, "You need to be in Sunday school, you need to be in church." Aunt Alice was always quoting Scripture to me, "the Bible says ...." Or "Jesus said..." so I was always ducking her. Even when I did go to church I sat somewhere in the back, trying not to be seen by them. But Aunt Alice would peer through the crowd to find me and then point me out, smiling and saying, to my dismay, "That boy back there, that's my nephew, let me tell you."

I didn't feel embarrassed in front of my friends though, because most of the time when I was in church my friends were *not*. I would squirm in my chair, silently urging, "Hurry up, hurry up. Hurry up praying, hurry up preaching, hurry up worship. Hurry up everything! I want to get out of here!"

My mom's way of making us go to church was to threaten. She told us, "Oh, you can't go to church, but now you want to go outside? That ain't happenin.' If you don't go to church, you ain't goin' out."

I went to church so I could hang out after our Sunday dinner. The way I'd get around my mom's rule was right before we got to the Center, my brothers and sisters and I would come to one of the little sidewalks that went off around the back, and that's where I would split off from them. Sometimes Aunt Alice would catch me before I could sneak away and make me come in. More often than not, though, she wouldn't, and my sisters and brothers would go on to church without me. My sister Angie would say, "You know you're supposed to be coming to church. I'm going to tell Mom."

I'd shrug. "Tell her."

One time when I was maybe thirteen years old my mom followed us. She let me go around the back of the church, and waited a few minutes.

I was back there, smoking and shooting dice, and I realized all the guys in the circle were looking at me funny. I was like, "What's with you?"

Finally, I turned around and saw my mom right in front of me. I saw the expression on her face and I knew it was going to be bad. My mom popped me right in the mouth. She slapped me, and the cigarette, the burning ember and everything, went all over my face. She asked, "What are you doin' down here? What did I tell you?"

After that, I was the laughing stock of our little gang. They'd laugh, "Remember dat time Moody mom came back here and slapped dat cigarette in his mouth? Dat boy look like a fire-breathin' dragon. He had fire comin' outta his mouth!" It took me a long time to live that one down. Those guys joked me out for years about that. "Remember dat time, remember dat time . . ."

5

Black and White

When I was around eight years old, something happened that, as I saw it then, made me realize a difference between blacks and whites.

My mom's grandmother was a slave, born in Virginia, back when plantations grew cotton, peanuts and tobacco. She worked in the house on a peanut plantation. Her daughter, my grandmother, ended up working for a white family, the Gibsons. She was their housemaid and nanny. She would clean up their house, wash and iron their clothes, and read stories to their kids. She became very close to the family. We were raised knowing that's who Grandmama worked for. As Grandmama got older, my mom took over for her.

One day, after my mom had been working for the Gibsons for a while, she took me to work with her because I was sick and she didn't want me to go to school, but she couldn't miss work.

We left our house, walked about half a mile to the bus stop, waited and caught the bus. We got off that bus and I thought we were there, but no. "We got another bus to catch," my mom told me. That bus was so hot it was hard to breathe. Finally, we got off the second bus and walked to the Gibsons' house about six blocks away.

Their dog was sleeping on their porch, and he thumped his tail as we walked past him to the front door. My mom rang the doorbell and a white woman opened the door to see me standing there with my mom. This white lady's face turned pale, then red. Her eyes opened wide and then narrowed. Her mouth twisted, and she spat out, "Why is he with you? He can't come in here. Why did you bring him? You need to take him home and you need to come back, because the work that has to be done has to be done." Then she called the dog inside.

That was the first time I made the distinction between the races. I thought, "Dogs get treated better than we do."

My mom and I had to walk back, catch the two buses, and walk home. She left me home alone, sick, and she went back to clean the Gibsons' house. Those people didn't want a black person, they didn't want *me*, in their house. My mom was black, but she was their housemaid—she was working for them.

That night my mom came home really late.

I never forgot that I was worse than a dog to that white family, and that's the way I pictured the black-white relationship. I kept that sentiment in my heart, and I grew to dislike white people because of that.

After that I was ticked off at the Gibsons, although the rest of my family loved them. However, when my mom died the Gibsons were there. My mom had helped raise those kids and they really loved her. She probably spent more quality time with them than she did with us. And they never forgot it; they gave me money towards my mom's funeral as well as a love offering. One of the Gibsons' grown children spoke at the funeral, recounting when my mom first started taking care of them. They also talked high about my grandma and the first time she came to their house, praising her commitment, dependability, and hard work.

I think the Gibsons were good people; I just didn't understand what was going on with black and white relations at that time. The incident at the Gibsons' front door happened in the early 1960s, when the civil rights movement was going on. Tensions were high. Now as I look back at that event, I realize Mrs. Gibson could simply have seen that I was sick and didn't want a sick kid in her house.

But after that day, I would see racism all the time. I looked for it.

When I was about fifteen years old my mom had the notion to get me out of the projects and get me squared away. She asked her older brother, James Council, Jr., to come and take me to live with him in Georgia. We called him Junie, short for Junior. When he came he said, "You're goin' with me and I'm gonna put you to work so you can understand what life is about."

While on our way we stopped at a gas station. We needed to get gas and use the bathroom. When we walked into the gas station's store we didn't see anyone. Junie called out, "Where your bathroom at?"

The guy working there was bent over, looking down, and he called out from behind the counter, "It's over there to the left, but you need a key to go in." Then he looked up and saw us. "You can't use the bathroom," he said. "I got no bathroom for you."

My uncle looked at me and said, "C'mon, don't worry about it. C'mon."

We bought the gas, but when we walked outside, my uncle said, "We good enough to buy the gas, but not good enough to use the bathroom." So my uncle and I went and peed on the side of the building. He made me pee on the side of that building.

Junie was in the army. He had a house right outside of Fort Benning, Georgia. He worked on the post during the day, and when he did come home at night he just figured me to be another guy. He'd say, "You gotta take care of yourself, you gotta watch out for yourself."

Junie still had his life. He'd come home with his girlfriend, or go see his girlfriend.

A couple times he took me to his girlfriend's house; she had twin daughters, and I was messing with both of them. It's unbelievable to me now how I went from bedroom to bedroom.

Junie gave me chores to do, and I would do them—I didn't want any problem with him. But once I had done what he asked me to do I'd hit the street. I was doing the same things I had been doing in Virginia: running with a bad crowd and getting into trouble. My uncle just didn't have the time to handle me; I was off-the-scales wild and didn't give a thought to what I was doing. I think I stayed in Georgia for less than thirty days. My uncle sent me back home on the bus.

That's just how I lived until I got so caught up in trouble that the police were looking for me. I was lying, stealing, cheating, manipulating, drugging. Even getting jailed didn't stop me.

6

In the System

One thing about the projects—there was just one entrance. One way in, and the same way out. I wonder now if that was strategic, built so nobody could go out a back way. Whenever the police made their daily showup somebody would holler out "PoPo" so you'd know—they're *here*. Then guys like me would hide out.

I was fifteen the day I first got caught. I had been a part of robbing people, and I had probably been on camera stealing from stores. I knew that the police had charges against me.

That day I heard the PoPo call, so I got away from the area because I thought they might be looking for me. I went to a different part of the project, in back, kind of like in the corner, thinking the police would ride through and ride out.

But on this day, they didn't.

They *were* looking for somebody; they were looking for a guy who had committed murder. Everybody knew he did it, and we all saw him around the projects, ducking and dodging when the police came through. They had his picture up in their car and they were on a manhunt for him.

There I was in the back side of the project and I thought everything was good; I thought I had gotten myself out of their scope. So I started heading back toward the front.

They pulled up on me out of nowhere. At first I was going to run, but I didn't.

They asked me where I was going, what I was doing. I told them, "Nothing." I did have some weed on me, which they found when they searched me. They handcuffed me, put me in the car and took me downtown to the police station and then to the Portsmouth City Jail. Going to jail that first time was the scariest thing I'd experienced. I really wasn't scared of the police; I was more fearful about where I was going. I was scared because of the unknown. People in the hood talked about going to jail, and I'd heard stories . . . there are a lot of fights and gang-related stuff happening in jail.

The police took my mug shot and fingerprinted me. Once I was in booking they told me they had several other charges: stealing and non-violent robbery, where I was part of a group that had robbed somebody.

Portsmouth City Jail was an adult jail, but they had a section for juveniles. If you were a juvenile you first went to the city jail, which was almost like a holding place to figure out where you were going to go. If you were looking at doing a longer sentence, they'd then place you in a juvenile detention center. I never went to one.

The police were polite that day. One officer said, "You know, we called your mom."

I was trying to be cool, so I shrugged and said, " . . . And?"

After I went through booking, a corrections officer walked me down the hall into my first holding cell and the officer shut the door. I heard the clang and then the solid click of the lock. That's when the reality set in. I knew I couldn't get out.

Three other guys were in there, one who looked older than me and two who looked my age. I didn't know them. They were from other projects, either Lincoln Park or Ida Barbour. They were talking but I didn't join in. One thing we didn't do is cross projects like that. I was nervous, but I stood apart from them, trying to look tough and act hard. Nobody hassled me.

The holding cell was maybe fifteen by eight feet, with concrete walls and floor painted gray. There were no chairs or beds. On one side was a metal bench the length of the cell. In the back was a stainless steel toilet. No divider or curtain. No privacy. If you had to use the bathroom in the holding cell, you had to do it in front of the other guys.

Right on top of the toilet was a little stainless steel sink. It wasn't an ongoing running faucet; it just gave a quick shot of water. You had to stand there and push, get one hand clean, switch, and get the other hand clean because the water stopped so quick.

The only time you're in a holding cell was while the staff was putting you in the system, giving you a number, figuring out where you were going to be located within the jail. I was in the holding cell for about four or five hours.

An officer came and brought me down a hall and up the elevator to the floor where juveniles were kept. The elevator door opened onto a hallway where I saw two pods, or dormitory-like areas, one to the right and one to the left. We turned and walked a few steps down the hall to the right. After about four or five feet the walls ended, replaced by iron bars running from the ceiling to the floor. In the center of the bars was the locked gate to the dorm, a single cell about thirty feet by twenty feet.

There were guys from different projects in there, plus some I knew from J-Dub. As we approached the dorm gate, they started hooting and hollering at me, "Hey, Moody Wop!"

That was my nickname, Wop. Some people might associate that with being Italian, but Wop was just the name my crowd had given me. "Wop" was whopping a person, punching a person. So Moody Wop identified me as a fighter. That name stuck with me until I got out of the cycle of in-and-out of jail.

Because I knew some of the guys in my cellblock, I started to feel less fear about being in there. But still, I felt like I had to be a big dude, I had to act tough. I had to show everybody that I could handle whatever came my way.

Five sets of bunks lined the back wall, and three sets of bunks filled the wall on the right side. There was a shower area with five spigots, like for PE in school. The water was hot; it was a good shower, and we could use it as often as we wanted.

Off center, in the open area of the cell, bolted to the concrete floor, sat two large round metal tables, each encircled by four metal stools also bolted into the floor. These walls, too, were gray concrete, tagged all over with stuff like, "Dog was here," and "Big Mike was here." The kids doing the tagging hadn't had paint or markers—they'd chipped off the concrete to form the letters.

In the back left corner, bolted to the wall, were the TV and telephone. A lot of fights went on over the phone.

In juvie we wore whatever we came in wearing. If somebody wanted to drop you off something, they could bring you a pair of jeans and a t-shirt, but no more than that. We weren't allowed to have more than two sets of clothes in the juvenile facility. When I was there, nobody brought me anything.

I started running with my mob, hanging out with the guys from my project. The guys from the other projects also hung out together. And we fought each other because we brought into the jail the beefs that we had out on the streets.

After maybe a week in there I went up before the magistrate. Because this was my first offense they didn't set bail. They just let me out and I was supposed to report to the probation officer. I figured jail wasn't so bad.

The worst part of being in jail came on the way home after jail. Sitting at the jail, waiting for my mom to take me home, I knew. I knew what was coming. And it did. My mom and my aunt picked me up, and my mom sat in the back seat with me while my aunt drove. My mom beat me all the way back to the house, talking all the while as she was busting me in the head: "*I (whap!) . . .*

*told (whap!) . . . you! (whap!) How . . . many . . . times . . .
did . . . I . . . tell . . . you?"*

I got my tail tore up. I got beat so bad it wasn't funny. I
was better off in the jail!

But that same night I went right back out in the street.
Being in jail, and my mom's beating me, didn't change
anything. I was just hardheaded and stubborn. I figured if
I could take that whipping from her, there wasn't too
much worse out in the hood that anyone could do, not
unless they shot me.

That's where the whole me being in the system began.
Now they had me on file with my mug shot and my
prints. The next time I was locked up, I was incarcerated
as an adult.

I see now all that mess, my behavior, and people's ways
in the projects, all that was moral bankruptcy. And that
moral bankruptcy was what made the projects, as that
graffiti writer said, "a hellhole." I saw a lot of terrible stuff in
the projects. But one thing really stands out.

7

Raw Project Life

The worst thing I ever saw in the projects happened during a craps game. Pretty much every day we shot craps, in different places all over the project. But most of our craps games took place behind the Center where the concrete parking lot met the dirt field. It wasn't unusual to see a group of guys all in a circle, up to eighteen guys shooting dice. On the ground there would be maybe fifty, or a hundred bucks total, split into different piles beside the players, who would be betting a dollar or a fifty-cent game.

One hot summer afternoon when I was seventeen, I was shooting dice with a bunch of guys. A couple of them were drinking out of cups from the bootlegger house. Off to the side of our circle a few guys were smoking weed, passing it, and it would come down into our circle. On the ground beside us we each had our packs of cigarettes, cans of beer, and our money pile. A radio was playing loud.

One of the guys, Harley, rolled and then rolled again, a seven, which meant he lost—he crapped out. He grabbed the pile of dollars beside him, saying it was his. But another guy, Slick, claimed it was *his* money. Slick said, "Man, you full of . . . You cheatin'! You got to give my money back." Oh, was he mad. Slick's veins were sticking out on the side of his head. And a big old argument broke out between them. Slick kept going on and on.

Slick was a good-looking guy, tall and slim. He was a manipulator, and smart, or *thought* he was smart. He was a thinker more than a brute force person. I never remember Slick being in a fight. He had like eleven brothers, and they looked out for each other. Nobody messed with him because they'd have a slew of brothers to mess with.

Harley was short, but he was solid, strong and thick. He was a bad dude; he was definitely a predator. Robbing, beating people up, manhandling, bullying, that was him.

Harley ended up holding the money. So Slick said, "You just wait right here."

I think everybody wanted to see Harley beat up Slick, because Slick was so smooth, such a ladies' man. Instead, Slick came back with a gun and blew Harley's brains out. The blood and brain tissue got on pretty much everyone in the circle, including me.

We knew Slick was mad, but nobody expected him to pull a trigger on Harley.

Harley lost his life over a couple dollars. I'll never forget it.

After Slick shot Harley everybody scattered. We all knew the police were going to be there soon. None of us was going to tell that Slick pulled that trigger. But somebody snitched—we never knew who. The police got Slick within two days. Slick was nineteen.

Slick is still in prison now. Not for this—he got out and robbed and murdered some insurance man. He went to prison for the second murder, got out, and robbed and murdered somebody else. He's got three bodies; he'll never get out.

To me, there was never any positive message in the projects. Even with Sunday school coming in and church being there, their impact was very, very superficial. We still shot, and partied, and fussed. They just had a Sunday school on that day in the midst of all this chaos. No way did I have any belief then that God really existed.

Like my dad I cycled in and out of jail several times. In between I continued another cycle I'd learned: broken relationships, and kids growing up without their dad. There was pain, but there would be healing, too.

8

Generational Healing

When I was twenty I went to Massachusetts trying to get away from the hood, not realizing it was in me. I had a cousin near Boston so I stayed with her. Though I got a few side jobs through her, mostly I continued getting into trouble.

I got my cousin's next-door neighbor, Sharon, pregnant. Sharon was just graduating from high school when I met her. We got married even though her mom was against it. I think Sharon felt getting married was the right thing to do. It wasn't so much me living right and being in love with her, because I wasn't living like that. My sinful nature was running me. Our son, Rashaud, was born in 1981 but I left soon after. Even though we were married, she gave our son her last name, not mine. She told our son that I was no good and for years Rashaud and I were estranged.

While I was in Massachusetts I joined the Army National Guard, but I ended up leaving the training. I was a rebel and didn't want to follow their orders. I didn't want to get up early for the training, and I got tired of the officers always on my back. I went AWOL. I got caught and sent to the army jail in New Jersey.

When I got out I first went back to Massachusetts, but later returned to New Jersey, where my dad and his sister were. When I arrived at night at the train station in Newark my dad met me and we rode to a stop near an apartment where there were a bunch of people. My dad led me to believe it was his place. I went to sleep and when I woke up my dad was gone, and the guy whose apartment it really was told me that my dad just showed up there once in a while.

I found my dad, and when I did rage flared up in me for him just leaving me there, and for all the times in my life he had never been there for me. I attacked him, landing punches. He defended himself and I backed off and left.

A few years after our fight my dad's girlfriend called to tell me he was sick and near death. He had been living on the streets, a heroin addict, and he had gotten pneumonia from exposure. I went to see him and he said to me, "I wasn't a good man, but I survived. You are like me; you're a survivor. Don't let anybody tell you you can't be whatever you want to be. You've got what it takes in you." I had never believed that, but he spoke life into me with those words, and it changed me. I stayed with my dad and was there the night he died.

Through my dad's girlfriend I met Karen, a woman she worked with. Previous boyfriends had abused Karen and when we met I stepped in to protect her. She, in turn, planted a seed in me to be a better person. She wasn't a party person, she kept her word, and she had a strong faith. We never married but we had a daughter, Vanisha. Karen died from cancer many years ago and I'm sad to say Vanisha and I haven't had a conversation since her mother passed. I am praying for healing in that relationship.

And though I had healed my relationship with my dad, it would be years before my son and I healed ours. Meanwhile, in the years after my dad died, I was still full of foolishness and sinfulness.

MEETING GOD AT THE BACK DOOR

9

Three Hots and a Cot

It took me several stints in jail to wise up. My last time in jail was in Courtland, Virginia, where this story began. The cellblock, or pod, had ten two-man cells. The cells were each about eight feet by five feet, with two bunks on one side and a toilet and sink on the cell's back wall. The shower was at the end of the cellblock. One showerhead for twenty guys.

Normally there were two guys in a cell but if the prison got overcrowded, you could have as many as two or three guys on the floor. The bunks were not regular beds; they were metal frames bolted into the wall. There was a thin plastic mattress—very thin—and a thin plastic pillow. When you got there, you got issued a pillowcase, a sheet and blanket, one towel and one bar of soap, and a roll of toilet paper. And that is the comfort of a jail cell.

For clothing the jail provided us with a top and bottom, like hospital scrubs; an undershirt and boxers, and flip-flops. Most of the time when we were in the block watching TV, playing cards and socializing, everybody wore just their boxers, flip-flops and white tees. We kept our scrubs for visitations. We "ironed" our scrubs by putting them under our mattress. That put a permanent crease in them.

In the block, the cells were all in a row, on the left. The door to the cellblock was never left open, but during the day the cell doors were unlocked. It was funny to hear an inmate say, "I'm going down to my buddy's house," when he meant walking the few short steps of the cellblock to his buddy's cell. Every night, lights went out at eleven; the cell door automatically slid closed and we were locked in overnight. The cell doors opened up again at six in the morning.

Along the length of the cells and in front of them was an open space about eight feet wide. This open common area was where guys worked out—doing crunches and push-ups, and where they walked back and forth down the pod when they didn't want to stay in their cell. That limited space was a high traffic area. The block was where all the fighting went down, where all the trouble happened, so we were safer when we were in the cell.

A solid concrete wall defined the common area, and in the center of the wall was an iron-barred metal door opening into the hallway. We could look through the bars and see that there were a couple of narrow, tall windows in the hallway, but we couldn't see directly out of them. Against the wall in the common area were little metal benches and a counter where we could sit and eat. Above the counter was a small rectangular opening large enough for the meal trays. At mealtime all the inmates stood at their cell or in their cell waiting for their number or name to be called. The guards would call us one at a time and slide our meal tray in. Once we had our tray we went back to our cell. All the meals had to be passed out before you could leave your cell and sit in the common area. Most of the guys just ate in their cell though, because out in the block a lot of the guys grabbed food off other guys' trays.

We got meals three times a day. "Three hots and a cot," that's what we called it in the jail.

You know how, when you're choosing a hotel, they list their amenities? Well, jail had amenities, too; we had canteen. Each floor got canteen on a different day. The canteen was actually a wheeled cart loaded with brown paper bags containing whatever each inmate had ordered the week before. Two food service people wheeled the cart into the block and they'd call our names one by one to get our bag.

Each week along with our bag we'd get an order form for the next week. The choices were stuff like cups of soup, packs of cookies, bars of soap, t-shirts and underwear.

We bought our stuff with credits from the work we did. We could get credits from other inmates as well as the jail. My dad earned credits drawing. The jail hired my brother Gerald as a barber. I wrote; I would write a letter for someone and get enough credits for four or five cups of soup.

We kept our canteen as close to us as possible, near or under our bunk, because people stole canteen constantly. They fought over it too. If an inmate was weak, his first canteen set the stage for what was going to happen from then on: he would be ordering for somebody else. And he had to order something, so the guys preying on him could take it.

We did have rec, or recreation, for an hour, a couple of days a week. The rec area had a pull-up bar and a square cement basketball court surrounded by dirt. Beyond the high chain link fence bordering the rec area we could see a view of some grass and then a wooded area. Everybody wanted that hour outside. If you didn't get in any trouble, you had rec; if you had some issues your rec was taken away.

The Television and the Telephone

Since the television was in the hallway, we had to watch it through the bars. To change channels, we either had to wait until an officer was out there, or we got creative: we made wands out of pages from someone's writing pad or newspapers that we rolled up very tight. We'd take the glue from the back of envelopes and stick it on the rolled-up papers and stick them together end-to-end. We made wands over a yard long that would fit through the bars to turn the TV on or off and change channels.

Inside the common area we had two telephones. As in juvie, lots of fights happened around the phone. The fights could get real bad, real quick. Inmates would often set a time for their people to call them. Some people in the pod, depending on how much power they had, or how popular they were, would try to take advantage of the phone. From time to time, though, their victims would just man up.

In one of my earlier times in jail as an adult, I was in with other guys from our project, including a guy called Hurricane. Hurricane had a rep as a bad guy out on the street, and he lived up to it. He could fight; he was really, really good with his hands. Out on the street, he also carried weapons. He was definitely a project hood; nobody was going to mess with him.

One Sunday, Hurricane was waiting for a call. Another inmate, a guy from Lincoln Park, was on the phone. When Hurricane thought his call was about to come in he said to the dude, "Look, Man, you need to hurry up with your call."

The dude looked at Hurricane and said, "Look, I'm on the phone. I get it, Hurricane, but ya know what I'm sayin'. I'm gonna get off when my time is done. I got five more minutes." And the dude stayed on.

Hurricane snatched the handset out of the dude's hand and started slamming the phone into the guy's head, opening his skull up. It didn't take long, about three whacks and the dude's head was split open.

Hurricane was about six feet two inches and muscular, just thick. The other guy was an average-sized guy, about five feet ten. But not only was Hurricane bigger; it was more than just his wanting to get on the phone—it was his releasing the anger in him.

The fight stopped when the guards came in and grabbed Hurricane and put him on lock in his cell. Then they made their report. They knew what had happened, but they had to go through their little routine, acting like they didn't know. They knew Hurricane. They weren't going to cross him, because he was one of those guys who would take on an officer in a minute, out of nowhere. By the time it's broken up, it's damage done. Hurricane might go to the hole, to solitary, but that officer would be beaten down.

Hurricane wouldn't have done that to me, partly because we were both from J-Dub. Plus, my sister and his sister were real tight, so we had a connection with our families. One night out in the hood Hurricane had saved me from a gunfight. That night I was so tired I couldn't even run. "C'mon, Man, c'mon, Man," he had said. And he had grabbed me and dragged me away.

When the Lincoln Park dude came back to our cellblock afterward he never had any problems with that phone. If Hurricane said, "Get off the phone," he said, "Hey, I gotta go." And he got off the phone.

I was moved to the work-release prison facility after I served ninety days my last time in jail. One of the criteria to be in the work release program is having less than a year left in jail. Work release meant we went out on work crews. We did stuff like picking up paper along the highways, or washing the patrol cars. Every day, Monday through Friday, we had a job. We'd go out at 8:00 a.m. and come in at 5:00 p.m., dinnertime. It was a good transition, a time to get used to being out of jail and in the community, keeping regular work hours. It was a better way to do time than sitting around doing nothing—or doing things you shouldn't be doing.

I was happy with the prospect of the additional freedom I would have there, and the knowledge that I was one step closer to getting out. I had no idea how much freedom I would really find there.

MEETING GOD AT THE BACK DOOR

10

Meeting God

It wasn't until that final time I was incarcerated that I began to even consider the notion of living a different life. And I didn't even really recognize it at first because I was like everybody else that was incarcerated; I was trying to be tough and trying to impress the other inmates.

The turning point was Kenny's study.

After moving closer and closer to Kenny's group, I actually went *into* the Bible study. I sat, I learned, and I began to ask questions about the Scriptures. I was beginning to see the difference between being a Christian and not being a Christian.

When I was in the Bible study with Kenny, I first heard the verses that have come to mean so much to me. They are the verses I put at the start of this book, Romans 12:1-2 (AKJV):

> I beseech you therefore, brethren, by the mercies of God, that you present your bodies a living sacrifice, holy, acceptable to God, which is your reasonable service. And be not conformed to this world: but be

you transformed by the renewing of your mind,
that you may prove what is that good, and
acceptable, and perfect, will of God.

These verses began to speak to my life. I started
studying them. It was a daily process for me, to dive into
that text. It came alive for me. I started to see myself in it.
And I think that's what empowered me to change, because
what the text is implying is to change ourselves, and thus
change our life, we first have to change the way we think.

Everyone else in Kenny's study was a Christian—they
had given their life to Christ and they were "saved." That
became the next step for me. Kenny prayed the sinner's
prayer with me and I accepted Jesus Christ as my Lord
and my Savior.

It struck me then that after all those years of people
trying to get me to know God in what you might call a
normal way . . . going to church, or accepting what people
were telling me about Him . . . I had finally met God—but
in jail. It felt to me like once again I hadn't taken the
simple way, the straight way. It felt like I had met God at
the back door.

I began to taste the freedom that comes with being
saved. It was just like Jesus told his disciples: "Everyone
who sins is a slave to sin. Now a slave has no permanent
place in the family, but a son belongs to it forever. So if the
Son sets you free, you will be free indeed" (John 8:34-36).

I began to want to do good, not to get out of prison
sooner, or to look good, or any reason like that. It was part
of the new identity I felt, part of the transformation I was
experiencing. I also made the choice to hang out with the

inmates in the church group and continue the Bible study with them.

Everybody in that block from J-Dub, we considered ourselves family. That was the first time they saw me begin to separate from the family. I was no longer a guy from J-Dub; I was a guy in the church group, where there were guys from Lincoln Park and from Ida Barbour as well as other guys from J-Dub. I stopped playing cards. I started reading my Bible. I got up early Sunday mornings to get a Christian channel on the TV, to hear a preacher preaching, some singing, or a church service. My selection didn't last long. When other inmates got up, they would switch the channel.

Soon after I accepted Christ an amazing thing happened.

MEETING GOD AT THE BACK DOOR

11

Kenny's Message

One night I thought I was dreaming because I saw Kenny come in my cell, talking to me. I couldn't really make out what he was saying. Surprisingly, it looked like he had a light on him. That's why I thought I was dreaming: because it was after lights out and the lights stayed off until the next morning. Not only that, but our cells were locked.

Kenny was telling me to lead the Bible study. And in the dream, I was telling him, "No, I don't think I'm ready, I don't think I'm the one. There's other guys in the group that can do it."

When I woke up the next morning, Kenny was gone. He had been released during the night. That's the way they do it most of the time in the system; they release the inmates at night or very early in the morning.

Kenny was gone and I didn't know if it was a dream or not. Maybe Kenny did come to my cell. I don't know, and I'll probably never know. All I know is there was an illuminating light around his face and he was telling me it was my place to lead the study.

I never connected with Kenny again. I hadn't paid attention to Kenny's last name, and unless God puts us together again, I didn't know, and still don't know, any way to contact him.

But from the day that Kenny left, I became the new leader of the Christian group we had on our block and for almost a year led morning devotions before we went out for work and Bible study in the evenings as well.

Leading the Bible study really changed my life. It changed how I interacted with the inmates. I'd hit up the new guys, invite them to Bible study. I wanted it to be welcoming for them, and not confusing. I remembered what it had been like for me when I had first heard Kenny and his group: they were talking about John, being in the Book of John . . . it was like Chinese to me. I mean John, Mike, Bill, whoever . . .

I tried to encourage others, like Kenny had. Kenny spoke life and strength into a dark place that was full of junk: the card games, the TV, the cussin' and the fussin'. I had to make a conscious choice to walk away from all that. In the cellblock we can always hear the TV but we can block that stuff out. When we grouped with our fellow believers, life was easier. We weren't an issue for the rest of the block unless they wanted us to be. Sometimes people who hated church stuff and church people came in and just wanted to start trouble.

Leading the study also changed how I interacted with the guards, or officers. Most of the officers dismissed us Christians, saying, "They'll be back after they get out." But some were like this one officer, a Christian, who told me, "When you get out, don't go back to where you came from." This officer was a big dude; he looked like a black Santa Claus, looked like he could eat a whole turkey in one sitting. I don't even know why they had him as a correctional officer—he couldn't run after anybody. He was a big teddy bear, so he really didn't have a relationship with the toughest guys. Instead he had a relationship with the guys that didn't fit in—guys that got beat up, guys that needed some encouragement. He was more of a YMCA Big Brother-type of guy, always laughing, joking, kicking it with the guys. He was a good guy.

He would give me Scriptures that addressed that issue of living a new way, like Romans 7:15-20:

> I do not understand what I do. For what I want to do I do not do, but what I hate I do. And if I do what I do not want to do, I agree that the law is good. As it is, it is no longer I myself who do it, but it is sin living in me. For I know that good itself does not dwell in me, that is, in my sinful nature. For I have the desire to do what is good, but I cannot carry it out. For I do not do the good I want to do, but the evil I do not want to do—this I keep on doing. Now if I do what I do not want to do, it is no longer I who do it, but it is sin living in me that does it.

The apostle Paul, author of the Book of Romans, walked me through a personal invitation of changing the way I thought. I no longer saw the Bible as a religious book but I started seeing the Bible as a living word for my life.

Another verse the guard gave me was Proverbs 3:5-6.

Trust in the Lord with all your heart
And do not lean on your own understanding.
In all your ways acknowledge Him,
And He will make your paths straight. (NASB)

The guard had connections in Charlottesville, Virginia. He wrote down a name and address and told me, "When you get out, make it to Charlottesville and see this guy, Mike, and tell him I sent you."

When I got out in February 1995 I did go back home to Portsmouth first. I went to see my mom and let her know I was going to Charlottesville. I didn't let anyone else know I was there. I knew one drink, one hit off a joint and I'd be right back where I started.

That in itself was a miracle: I went back to the project for that visit and I didn't go back to my old ways. I had no idea of the miracles ahead of me in Charlottesville.

*But you should put aside from you your first way of life,
that old man, which is corrupted by deceitful desires, and
you should be made new in the spirit of your minds.*

—*Ephesians 4:22-23 (ABPE)*

12

Go Ye into the House of the Lord

I got off the bus I had taken to Charlottesville and walked to the Salvation Army. I told them I had recently been released from jail and needed a place to stay. Before I could stay they told me to go to the sheriff's department to fill out a form.

When I brought the form back to the Salvation Army they took me in and gave me room and board.

After I got that taken care of and I knew I had a place to stay, I walked through Charlottesville, heading down Main Street. A sense of a different sort of reality was setting in. I was no longer incarcerated. I was free. I was out.

That Old Man, He Was Still in Me

Yes, I was out. But I wasn't really free yet. All those desires, that old man, he was still in me. As I was walking down Main Street, I could see a liquor store coming up. And there was something in me that wanted to go and get a bottle of liquor. I had maybe ten dollars on me, so I had the money for it.

It was like everything just started raging up in me—the way I used to think, the way I used to carry myself. I started looking at the women that I was passing in the street, kind of intensely looking at them, as I was coming up on this liquor store. I got about ten feet away from that liquor store, and stopped.

My thought was to go in and grab a bottle of liquor. I put my hand in my pocket to get my money and pulled out a copy of *Our Daily Bread*, a little paperback devotional I'd been given in the jail.

Glancing at it, I read the cover title: "Go Ye into the House of the Lord."

Clutching that booklet, I looked again down the street. Now I noticed that just past the liquor store was the First Baptist Church of Charlottesville, and between them was a storefront, with big glass windows on either side of the glass entry door with a sign that read, "First Baptist Church Main Office." Instead of going in the liquor store I went past it, into the church office.

A short, stocky woman was sitting at a desk over on the right side. When I opened the door, she looked up. "Come on in," she said with a nice big smile. She got up, tugging on the bottom of her pantsuit jacket to straighten it. Beside her desk were some big file cabinets and a potted plant. There was a loveseat too. Some pictures were on the wall. The place looked comfortable, inviting.

I told the secretary a little bit of my story, that I had just gotten out of jail and was living in the Salvation Army, and I really wanted to talk to the pastor.

She told me, "Really, Sir, he's doing his last session for the day, his last interview with a member, and he won't be able to see you today."

I persisted. "Look, Ma'am, I really need to talk to a pastor."

"He's doing his last meeting now, and he really doesn't have another slot."

"I really need to see a pastor, I need to talk to someone," I said. "I really need to talk to him because I'm feeling confused." That notion to drink and look at women, it was just raging in me.

Finally she said, "Let me call over there." She phoned his office and explained to him what I had said.

The pastor told her to send me over.

The secretary directed me around the corner to the church, a big brick building, and to the pastor's office, which was under the church.

I got to the door and rang the bell. Questions raced through my mind: Would I make a bad mistake, a wrong move? Would I give in to the temptations? Then the pastor opened the door.

Reverend Bruce Beard was a slim man, a light-skinned brother, about five feet nine inches tall, wearing slacks and a button-down shirt with the sleeves rolled up. He had a close-shaven beard. I guessed he was in his forties, a few years older than me. He smiled, his whole face gentle, warm and open. His hair, wavy, not curly, was cut short. He had one striking feature: just off center, where his hair parted, he had a stark white streak. You could tell when someone dyed their hair; this was natural. Later I learned he'd had it from birth.

The reverend invited me in and we entered what looked like a waiting room. There was a coat rack and a small polished wood table with a Bible on it. Down a hall I could see the stairs that led up to the sanctuary, and a sign for a men's and women's bathroom.

He said, "Let's go back to my office."

He led me down the hall, across their Fellowship Hall to the end of the room, and through the door into his spacious office. I saw a big polished dark wood desk, a dark bookcase going all the way to the ceiling, and burgundy upholstered chairs with nailhead trim. It all looked dignified, comfortable and welcoming. Peaceful.

He sat down. I stayed standing. As I stood there . . . I experienced something I had never felt in my life: that feeling that I had about drinking and women, I felt it just drop. I didn't want to leave.

I sat then and we talked for the next hour. I told him my story. Then he said, "I'm glad you stopped by the church. I know how tough it can be when you first get out." He gave me a warm invitation to come to the church service, without judging me.

Then, after I had just told him about my getting out of jail and my temptation with the liquor store, he put a ten-dollar bill in my hand and told me, "Come back tomorrow."

And that's what I did. I went back to the Salvation Army, got myself situated for the night, and the next day I went back to that church.

That day began what has been my more than a twenty-year walk with God as a free man. Every day Rev. Beard would tell me, "Come back the next day; come back the next day."

Little did I know where that daily choice would take me.

MEETING GOD AT THE BACK DOOR

13

A Pastor's Discipleship

Reverend Beard started ministering to me. He took me on under his wing and started counseling me. He literally gave me the key to that church and made me the volunteer janitor.

I couldn't see it then, but when I look back on it now, I see how God was using him in my life. Giving me that key became critical to my transformation process. There were people at that church that had been there forty years that didn't have a key to the church. But here I was, a guy that had just gotten out of jail, and the pastor turned over the key to the church to me.

I also connected to the guy the prison guard had told me to contact, a guy named Mike. Through Mike I got a job doing janitorial work at the University of Virginia, but I didn't stay long. It wasn't the work; I was doing the same kind of work at the church. I just felt there was something else for me.

Every day I was at that church, vacuuming, cleaning the toilets, doing all the jobs a janitor or sexton would do.

As I was in the church, counseling with the pastor, and dealing with my issues, sometimes I found myself using my key to the church just to be there; at times it felt like a raft I was clinging to, hanging on for my life. I was dealing with my demons, that drug demon, that perverted demon, and all the other demons that had a hold on me the first part of my life. They hadn't gone anywhere; they were still there.

I was finding out that living at the Salvation Army was challenging. In some ways, living there was like going from jail to work release. We still had chores, we still had bed count, and we had to be in by a certain time. We had a lot of things we couldn't do. It felt like I had had more freedom in jail than I had in the Salvation Army. And it was a dorm setting, with bunks, even closer in the Salvation Army than in the jail.

To be blunt, the air felt pretty close too. In jail, if a dude stunk, the inmates would throw him in the shower clothes and all, and maybe beat him up, too. That wasn't happening at the Salvation Army.

The Salvation Army is a Christian organization. This one was a freestanding brick building with a church in the front. It was connected to a back building that housed the homeless and the people that needed shelter, but we couldn't get to the shelter from inside the church. The only ones who went through the building to the shelter were the Salvation Army employees.

The shelter had a little central area where we checked in, and a cafeteria. The dorms for women were on one side, and the ones for men on the other. A chain link fence, about eight feet high, enclosed the whole building and parking lot. Surveillance cameras were mounted on top of the fence, and the gate was locked at night. Unless we had a really good reason, if we didn't get in by the set time, we were out until the next day.

The Salvation Army provided breakfast, lunch, and dinner. A lot of times I would walk back for lunch from the church. It was only a ten-minute walk, just across some railroad tracks. We didn't have to pay, but for us to have that food and hang on to that bed we were encouraged to search for work and find a job. At the shelter we each were on the chore list, with rotating jobs.

One week it might be cleaning the kitchen floor, the next week it could be cleaning up the parking lot, or cleaning the dorm. A Salvation Army major oversaw the daily operations. We each had a case manager. David, my case manager, was the director of the shelter, and their social services person.

Part of the challenge of living at the Salvation Army was some of the guys there were drinking cheap liquor, getting high with weed, crack, and the most common—crack cocaine. They were using stuff that makes a guy get crazy and fight, stuff that makes him get thrown out of the Salvation Army. I saw the police get called and guys ending up going back to jail. The Salvation Army was in the pocket of poverty, in the projects, and drugs were all around. For me, part of the problem was the staff knew what was going on and didn't deal with it.

Despite the fence and the security, the stuff went on. Behind the shelter building, behind the parking lot, was a little wooded area. People would do their stuff in the back, in the dark, at the fence corners. The cameras faced the back of the building. They filmed the doors, the kitchen entrance, the living areas, the offices. But as far as the fence line, back there . . . nothing.

Whenever I felt temptation or pressure about the stuff going on in the Salvation Army, I got Rev. Beard to okay my being at the church for the night. Those nights I spent cleaning like a madman. It was good to be out. I wasn't locked up. I had the freedom to be over that whole building with nobody telling me when to go to bed, nobody telling me when to get up. The work, the freedom, they were a joy to me.

Usually, those guys at the shelter that wanted to do their thing, they didn't mess with me. But I still felt tempted anyway. I mean the taste of the cocaine; at times I wanted to do it again.

One Saturday, after I'd been at the church for about five months, I came really close to doing cocaine again and getting back into the drugs. There was a group of three guys at the shelter. They were getting high, doing what I used to think was a good time. I knew it was really killing them, but even so, there was a part of me that really wanted to indulge in it that night.

Instead, I went in the shelter office and I told the desk manager that I had—and I did have it—permission to go to the church. It was me running away from the devil. I had never felt the devil pursuing me like I felt him that night.

I got in that church and I didn't do one bit of work. I went right inside that church sanctuary and I cut off every light that was in there, and I lay in the fetal position like a baby, on the carpet, right there in front where the stage goes up and the pastor's podium is. I lay there that night and I cried and cried, and cried out to God.

I could hear the demons after me, even there, in the sanctuary. They wanted me back. Thoughts came to me like, "I don't have to be here; I can get high. I can do whatever I want to do. I'm not locked up anymore."

I began crying out Scriptures. I wasn't as well versed as I am now, but there were a couple I knew that were just what I needed right then. I took Isaiah 54:17 and made it personal for me: "No weapon formed against me will be able to prosper."

Then it was like someone was talking to me, trying to persuade me: "You can go hang out all night; you can go get sex; you can go get drugs. Nobody will know. Just come back in the morning and go to church." I was sweating, sweating profusely, and feeling like I could taste the drugs. It was crazy.

The devil wanted me back. I wasn't going back. I said aloud, "The devil's 'a liar and the father of lies.'" I cried out, "Greater is He that's in me than he who is in the world." I was saying, "Lord, Your Word says I'm more than a conqueror," and, "If You are for me who can be against me?"

Still, thoughts ran wild in my head: "I'm already out of the Salvation Army; I got an excuse for the night."

In answer, over and over I kept repeating those power Scriptures of His Word, of who we are. I spoke the promises God gave me that I had learned to quote and put in the atmosphere. I said, "The enemy doesn't have any power over me." I clung to God and His Word, saying, "God, 'close the doors man can't open.'" I wasn't shouting the words; I was speaking them into the atmosphere. It was a whisper. It was enough that I could hear it. And the enemy could hear it.

I heard the Holy Spirit, too. Holy Spirit spoke to me, saying, "Rest, you can make it through this." Holy Spirit's words were soothing, coming on me like a healing balm. With every attack on me, Holy Spirit spoke an answer: "Don't get up; don't leave. Don't go out the door; don't even move. Stay right here and fight."

Because it really was a fight. My body was fighting. I look back at that night and realize some kind of spiritual detox happened. It wasn't a lot of praying; it was more just being in God's presence. After several hours I fell asleep. I woke up the next morning and I knew I was done. Since then, though there were times when temptations came, I would remember this night when God delivered me. I became a lot more confident and more bold in my relationship with God.

Serving the Lord

Ever since I had arrived, Rev. Beard and I had been meeting weekly in his office. I was also at his house a lot. The parsonage, the church-owned pastor's home, was maybe a mile and a half away from the church. At first I was driven there in the church van or the Salvation Army's. Later I drove myself.

Rev. Beard and his wife, Gardenia, also a pastor, had never had kids. The church family was their family.

Because I was with him so much I was beginning to understand ministry. I saw how taxing it is and how spiritually draining it was for him to minister to a congregation of broken people and still have a life. I got to see how he dealt with spiritual attacks, see him walk with the love of God. I saw his wisdom and I saw the strength it took and from him I learned how to respond. I also became like his armor bearer, doing what I could to lighten his load. I basically became a part of his household. I took his clothes to the cleaners. I washed his car. I mowed his lawn. I would do landscaping and all kinds of stuff.

When I had been involved with the church for almost a year, the church janitor left.

He was responsible for vacuuming and cleaning the church building, and picking up church members on Sunday in the church's big twelve-passenger van. When he left, I got the position and the pay, and worked as the church janitor for several years.

Under the pastor's leadership, I went from a janitor to an usher at the front doors of the church, then to a Sunday school teacher, first teaching kids, then teens, and then adults. For the first time in my life, my focus wasn't doing a job to get money for drugs but doing the job to serve the Lord.

Early on, I could never understand the text that said, "If anyone is in Christ, he is a new creature; the old things passed away; behold, new things have come" (2 Corinthians 5:17 NASB). I had been operating in the sinful me, the old me, the me that didn't have a relationship with Christ; the me that didn't desire a relationship with Christ; the me that did not know how to have a relationship with Him.

I didn't know how to change, either. Romans 12:1-2 enlightened me on that. Through everything, that Scripture resounded in my life.

> I beseech you therefore, brethren, by the mercies of God, that you present your bodies a living sacrifice, holy, acceptable to God, which is your reasonable service. And be not conformed to this world: but be you transformed by the renewing of your mind, that you may prove what is that good, and acceptable, and perfect, will of God. (AKJV)

My whole life was changed on that text. That text literally came alive to me; it helped me understand what it was to be in that transformation process.

That word, *transformation*, is similar to the Greek word *metamorphosis*, which is used to describe the process of the caterpillar turning into a butterfly—two creatures in one. I saw there was another me in me. And there is another *you* in *you*.

We humans are changed by the renewing of our minds, by changing our thinking. Romans 12:1-2 is the basis of the whole prison ministry I lead now; it's the basis of my sharing with other men and women that their lives can be different if they learn to change the way they think. That's what the Scripture says to do.

I have learned our transformation as Christ followers is never completed. There will be times when temptations come but temptation will get less and less and the victories we have in one area will transfer to other areas.

Ministry Growth

After I had served under Rev. Beard for over a year I was ordained as a deacon. This was a huge step for me. It was the first acknowledgment of the changes in my lifestyle and character. In my early life I had always centered on impressing people from the street and living up to the expectations of the world. For the first time I felt part of the body of Christ and I was honored to be recognized as a servant of God.

Rev. Beard would encourage me. "I'm telling you, you will always be fine because I see you putting in the work," he'd say. "I've had people here with me for almost twenty years that haven't walked as much as you've walked."

"Putting in the work" was leading early morning meetings for months at a time. It started with Rev. Beard and meetings he led at the church. He taught me how to teach and encourage the participants and I ended up running early morning Bible studies both inside and outside the church.

I led different groups, people from the Salvation Army and the community—people in recovery, the lost. At 6:00 a.m. at the Salvation Army we'd just pull chairs from the shelter out into the parking lot, form a circle, and meet there, men and women. Mostly though I led groups of guys. We met in different community centers in housing projects in Charlottesville, one on Monday, another one on Thursday. My schedule was rigorous.

Rev. Beard counseled me every day, and I would pour into the men what he would pour into me. That's what Christ said in Matthew 28:19-20: "Go, disciple people in all nations, baptizing them in the name of the Father and of the Son and of the Holy Spirit, teaching them to obey everything that I've commanded you." (ISV)

To communicate to the men what discipleship really is, I'd tell them what Rev. Beard always told me: it takes a disciple to make a disciple. Disciple is the base word for discipline. All Christ was saying was something like this: "I'm not asking you to go and make holy people, 'cuz you can't do that. I'm the only one that can do that. I am Christ alone.

"However, I want you to go by example and show people how to live disciplined lives, because the disciplined lives will bring them in line to hear the truth and the truth sets them free."

Rev. Beard taught me that for my life. And it worked. The key is deciding to stop covering up the truth and instead walk in the truth—and this sets us free. The guys I was dealing with in these drug-infested places weren't dealing with the truth. Guys in this lifestyle, we deal with cover-ups and lies. We all did. But it wasn't until I was strong enough and not intimidated by the truth that I could say, "Hey, that's me. I did that."

Some people might look at what I had done in my past and say, "That's terrible." That old stuff, that's who I used to be. That's not who I am now. I can be honest and tell it because I know God loves me and God is changing me. And I know there's power in the testimony. Philippians 1:12 says, "Now I want you to know, brothers and sisters, that what has happened to me has actually served to advance the gospel." And Psalm 22:22 says, "I will praise you to all my brothers; I will stand up before the congregation and testify of the wonderful things you have done." (TLB)

These things Rev. Beard showed me about power and the testimony and about making a disciple I poured into the men. I didn't have to be a rocket scientist; I just had to be faithful to God's Word.

God began blessing me in so many ways. In 2000, in addition to my work with Rev. Beard and First Baptist, I began training and working with a program for dual-diagnosed individuals, people with psychological and addiction issues. I was the resident manager at one of the program's homes in Charlottesville, taking the guys to counseling appointments, dispensing their meds, making sure they were in the house. Not only was it room and board for me but they also paid for me to get one year of drug counselor training on weekends—in Virginia Beach.

I got to see my mom nearly every weekend. She was very glad to see my life change. It blessed me for her to see me different. I told her, "I am so sorry. I know I was terrible."

She agreed, "Yeah, you was the most rebellious kid I ever had. But one thing about you, if you said you was gonna do something, you did it. Even if it was wrong. You got to where you'd say, 'Hey Mom, I'm gonna stay out all night.'" She said, "I'm so glad you turned your life around. I'm proud of you."

That was the last year she was alive. She was in the hospital for a while, but she had so much trouble there, we ended up bringing her home in hospice care. When she died in 2001, a bunch of the family were in the house, and we could all sense it was time. That last day with my mom everybody was happy that she was home, rather than in a hospital. She had said her goodbyes the day before, and now although she was conscious, she wasn't talking much. She was such a loving mom. The talking she had done was telling everybody how proud she was of them. Three of my sisters and I were in her room with her when she passed. She took a breath and then she stopped breathing. It was really hard for all of us in the room.

My brother Gerald was locked up when our mom died. I had tried, without success, to get him a furlough to come see her. But we did get him a furlough to come to the funeral. Two guards brought him in, let him see her, and then took him out. We knew he had shackles on his ankles and handcuffs on his wrists, but one officer had draped his jacket over the handcuffs so we couldn't see them. Seeing him there like that was an enormous blow. Before he got in the car to return to jail I told him, "Look, I'm going to help you."

At that time, I hadn't yet visited him. My mindset had been jail wasn't a place I wanted to be. I didn't want to go back to jail, not even to visit. Not anybody.

But after the funeral I visited Gerald twice before I went back to Charlottesville. I told him, "You can't keep living like this. You've gotta get out of this cycle; you've got to change your life."

I suggested a plan to get him out of J-Dub and the project mindset. "When you get out, get your parole and probation address transferred to Charlottesville." So we worked on that and he came to Charlottesville. I gave him six months to stay with me, get a job, open up a bank account, and get out of that cycle.

He never went back to the project. That was his last time in jail, too.

He stayed with me for eight months. At that time I wasn't yet a pastor, but I was in the church heavy and I was on fire for God. I was really preaching at him now.

He said, "Man, I really want to change."

I told him, "I can help you. I can't help you be a man, but I can give you a hand. Not a handout, but a hand, to help you. But it's really got to be what you want to do. You know what I mean?" I told him I didn't want him to be drugging and stealing and taking from me because of the addictions.

"You know it, I know it, you know I know it. You don't need that stuff. I'm presenting you the opportunity to change. You saw me sell it; you saw me do it for years, and look at me now."

Even though he was not yet out of the cycle, he was responsive enough to my support to feel like I wouldn't let him down. Our conversations were good. This was the big pivot for him, and for us as brothers. He knew he could depend on me.

Still, his road wasn't easy and he had his own turns and detours.

What finally happened was he went to live with one of his best friends from the project, Mario. He and Mario had run together, drugged together, done everything together. And while Gerald was locked up, Mario got robbed and shot and was now permanently in a wheelchair, living in North Carolina. For a time Gerald stayed with Mario there, and something changed.

When he came back from Carolina, Gerald started going to church with me every Sunday. He wouldn't miss even one. He got to know the pastor, and he stuck close to me. He said, "I want to be like you. I want to know the Lord . . . I want to be like Christ."

Gerald eventually settled in Texas, and got a good job as a cook at a university there. He likes to eat, he likes to cook, and he can really do both.

He's a Christ follower to this day. He never looked back. That doesn't mean there are no challenges; no, there are plenty of challenges for anybody who decides to follow Christ. What I went through next shows you that.

14

Growing . . . Mistakes . . . Getting Back up

It was April of 2001 when my mom died. I missed her deeply. Soon after, I met a woman during a revival meeting that was traveling through different churches. She and I married a few months after my mom's death. We stayed married for almost ten years. We had no kids. I wanted to stay married and worked on the marriage for years. We were both Christians, but her church taught religion rather than relationship. What I mean by that is relationship with God is developed by speaking and listening to God and doing what He says. Religion is following a set of rules and expecting that God will then deliver. It's like God is a vending machine.

It was my relationship with Christ and God meeting me where I was that had freed me; I could never replace that with religion. Over the next ten years my wife and I would discuss this difference, but I never really felt heard until she asked for a divorce.

In 2011 she said to me, "I believe it wasn't God's will for us to be married."

I answered her, "Really, it is your will that we get divorced."

Though it was not my choice, we separated. I paid her rent so she could save up money and the divorce was finalized later that year. It was important to me that I support her until she could make it on her own. I didn't want any bitterness between us.

Getting My GED

For years, the Bible studies I had been teaching, first in jail and then in Charlottesville, had been raising questions in me. The more I taught, the more I wanted to know. But to get the depth of understanding I wanted, I really needed to go to seminary. I was a high school dropout. I needed a GED.

In 2005 I went to get my GED at the Charlottesville Adult Learning Center and I failed the test the first time because I failed the math. When I was going for my GED it was difficult. In the morning I was still leading Bible studies with guys at the Salvation Army and around the community, and I was being accountable, but that old world was still all around me. Daily I needed to make the choice to be different and follow God. And I did.

I was reading my Bible, but it wasn't just me opening up my Bible, it was the Word becoming a part of who I was. I was in the church as often as I could be there. One of the members of First Baptist, a math professor, tutored me for the part of math that was giving me problems. I hadn't learned it in high school; mostly I had gone to my high school to deal, steal, fight, and cause trouble. The second time I took the GED test I passed it.

I hadn't realized the doors it would open up, but God did. I went to qualify for seminary and God blessed me with much more. I was learning discernment, finding my path, and learning along the way—often from my many mistakes. Through my wife's former boss I got a job with a temp agency working as a Xerox technician. I worked in one tall building with many floors, maintaining all the copy machines there. I did well at the work, and was developing a good track record: being on time, keeping my word, and being careful to complete every bit of a task. I began to envision a future with this work. Xerox liked what I was doing and wanted to hire me away from the temp agency. They offered me a permanent position and a raise. In the process they also did a background check—and when the results came back with my prison record, they fired me.

I was crushed.

Then God spoke to me, "Get up, you've got to have faith in me. Xerox didn't bring you this far, I did. Focus on me being your provider. You've been walking, growing in the Holy Spirit. Don't give up just because you lost this job. I'm doing something with you."

I realized God's plan for me wasn't about companies or machines, it was about me working with people rather than machines. And I began to see God's provision. During this time I had a car I was making payments on.

After I lost my job I lost the car because I couldn't make the payments. But then someone gave me a car. Also, as I was ministering to people, I would find in my mailbox money that people had anonymously given me.

For a time I still worked part-time as the church janitor and eventually I worked with the elderly at the John Jay Brain Center in Charlottesville. Working there prepared me for the real close quarter work that you do with the elderly, washing their bodies, cleaning them, and doing whatever they couldn't do for themselves. It became a blessing to me to be able to help people that way.

Going to Atlanta in 2008

In January of 2008 I was ordained through Rev. Beard's First Baptist Church. Shortly after, Rev. Beard, his wife, and about ten families moved to Atlanta to plant a new church, Transformation Ministries. Rev. Beard wanted to go a new way in ministry, similar to how he had discipled me. I was still married then. I got my wife settled in an apartment in Atlanta, but I stayed in Charlottesville to finish school.

I never got a bachelor's degree, but with all the community college courses I had taken and all the classes I had taken as an intern in Charlottesville I was accepted in 2006 into Virginia Union University's three-year master's degree program in Richmond. To stay in this master's program, we had to have a certain grade average after the first year. I had above average grades so I didn't have a problem.

That three-year program was very challenging. The first year I slept in my car. The second year I roomed with another guy in the program, and the third year my cousin let me stay at his place, but that was often in his garage. All three years I was doing a lot of driving between Richmond and Charlottesville, and the last year and a half, as I helped Rev. Beard transition to Atlanta, I added driving to that city. With all that driving I didn't have money for rent for myself.

Although I was still working as the church janitor, I finished before a lot of my class because I had taken summer classes in addition to the regular school year. It was amazing to me that I was the one who came in with a GED and I ended up at the top of my class. I moved to Atlanta to be with my wife, but in May of 2009 I went to Richmond and, walking with my class, I got my Master of Divinity degree from Virginia Union University.

My first time speaking from the pulpit was in Atlanta at Rev. Beard's Transformational Ministries church. If they were traveling, or he was ill or took a sabbatical or a break, I would fill in. I preached on a fairly regular basis. My title wasn't assistant or associate pastor. With black churches, it's Reverend. I was always addressed as Reverend Moody. But I never took payment as a pastor with Rev. Beard. For income I worked as a chaplain.

In 2010 I interned in a continuing education program for work as a chaplain through the Henry Medical Center in Stockbridge, Georgia. In 2011 I interned as a chaplain in Portsmouth, Virginia, at Newport News Hospital, where I was born, and got my chaplaincy certificate. That same year I got my certificate of ordination from Transformation Ministries in Atlanta, so I was now ordained as a minister in two states.

I tried starting a prison ministry in Georgia, going in as a chaplain with the support of Transformation Ministries, but I didn't have men to follow me and I wasn't successful there. Even though I was doing what I believed I was supposed to do, the doors were closing.

One of the things that Rev. Beard and I both knew was that God was preparing me for something that wasn't in Charlottesville and wasn't in Atlanta. We didn't know where it was, but we knew it was a time of preparation.

Rev. Beard will always be my spiritual father, but our time together came to an end one day in the fall of 2012. We met together in his office before service started. He was still encouraging me, saying things like, "I am so proud of you and how far you've come; and I'm looking forward to the great things you're going to do through God." I couldn't see if he was crying because I was crying so much. I was leaving my best friend. He had already prepared the congregation that this was my last time to deliver the message and that I was moving to Florida.

I ministered and allowed God to use me. Do I remember what I said? No, I was too emotional. That last sermon I preached there was in September 2012. I was fifty-four years old. And I was starting over.

15

Starting Over

A friend had recommended I move to Florida's Sarasota-Bradenton area and recommended a church there, too. The year before I settled in Florida I had traveled to Bradenton and visited the church. When I walked in the door at Bayside Community Church, I knew this was where I was supposed to be.

Bayside is one of the fastest growing churches in America. One of the reasons for that is the vision and leadership of Senior Pastor Randy Bezet. Pastor Randy says, "Bayside exists to reach people for Christ, raise them to be followers of Christ, and release them into their God-given purpose."

Now—I had arrived. I went to Bayside's main campus in Bradenton at first. Soon after, the church launched their East Sarasota Campus. Since I had rented a room with a husband and wife who lived closer to Sarasota, I was a part of that launch.

The first time I came to Bayside's East Sarasota Campus I knew that this was the Bayside location for me. That first day I met the campus pastor, Craig King, and I asked for an appointment to let him know my history. When we had our meeting, within the next week or so, I told him I was very interested in Bayside's leadership track.

One of the things Rev. Beard taught me about ministry and leadership is serving and making sure things are always in order. So, one of the first things I wanted to do was come up under the authority of Pastor King. Even though I had already been preaching and had pastoral degrees in two states, I did that. Starting out at the bottom for me was greeting out front.

Every since my salvation in the jail, I have felt compelled to welcome people into the house of God. Love on 'em, invite 'em, and welcome 'em. Even before I was on a greeter or service team, I stood outside the church doors and welcomed people. I walked my way from this to being ordained as one of Bayside's pastors.

I understood that as an ex-felon I needed to earn people's trust, that I had to *show* them, not *tell* them, and that would take time. Four years later, at his presentation to the church family when he ordained me, Pastor King commended me for that. He said, "This man's older than me, he holds a degree, but he submitted to my authority."

Some people hide their history. But my experience with Xerox gave me a clear sense that as I follow God's path for me, He wants to use *all* of me. Once again I realized God had blessed me with a testimony. My experience of being incarcerated glorified God. Instead of trying to cover that up, I shouted it out. It was in jail that

Kenny led me to Christ, and in jail my personal relationship with Jesus Christ grew. When I got out of jail, the power in my witness was about being in jail. I took it as a positive.

I'm sure especially initially some of the people in the church might have felt or even said, "This guy's talking and going on about being a felon!" But that's my point: This is what God did; this is what God can do in the life of a felon—or anyone else. He can take you out, get you a master's degree, put a Word in your heart . . . and send you out to preach!

I came to Florida with the same drive and desire I'd had in Georgia and Virginia: get in the jail and prison system and share the gospel. I started volunteering as a chaplain at Sarasota County Jail. Chaplains in jails and prisons get called when someone loses a family member or when someone's on suicide watch. Also, at some point most guys and women that are incarcerated simply want to talk to a chaplain about their issues.

At the same time, I began volunteering with hospice as a chaplain. One of the main reasons I came to Florida was because it was a state of retirees and elderly. I thought my plan to work in hospice was kind of good: I had training, I had certifications, and I had done chaplaincy work. I had my portfolio filled up with pastoral care, clinical setting. I was getting myself established but it was all volunteer. I still needed a job to put a roof over my head.

But hospice would not hire me. I wondered if it was because I was black. I had the credentials but others would get hired over me. I wondered if it was because I was an ex-felon. Until people saw the fruit of my labor they generally did not trust me. I knew guys like me have a lot to prove.

I was lamenting and going on, crying and looking for work, volunteering at the jail, volunteering in hospice. I was burning myself out. Doors were shutting. My savings were disappearing. I think now that God wants us to realize that He is in the midst of our journey, but we still have to go through that journey.

Money became a challenge; the place I was living became a challenge. I was paying $500 a month for a room. The couple I rented from was very frugal: I would put my clothes in the washing machine and they would take them out, saying, "You can't wash on the weekend." If I went in to take a shower, the husband would say, "Moody, you know, you're running a lot of water." They took their showers at the gym where they worked out.

My lowest point came the day I needed to pay the rent and I didn't have enough money. What I did have was a beautiful white gold man's watch my mom had gotten from a family member. I don't think it was an heirloom, but she had given it to me right before she died. I also had a gold chain she had given me. That watch and chain were my connection to my mom and I knew if I pawned them I wasn't going to get them back.

I sat on my bed at that house, holding that watch and chain, thinking I would pawn them and go back to Georgia or Virginia. I almost gave up. I was at my wits' end. No doors were opening. I cried out to God, " I don't know how much of this I can take. If this is not where I'm supposed to be, let me know." I was definitely in the mindset of leaving. I was doubting that the decision to come to Florida was God's will, and Holy Spirit wasn't saying anything. I pawned my mom's gifts and paid my rent.

The very next Sunday at church one of the members, a sweet lady named Miss Cherry, came up and asked, "What is going on with you? You're just not yourself. You're not happy."

"I don't know . . . I don't know," I muttered. "I don't know if I'm doing stuff in my own strength."

She said, "How can I help you?'

"I don't know. I don't know where I'm going to live. . . ."

Miss Cherry said, "I have a place."

And that was the beginning of my coming out of the wilderness, of coming out of that desert place.

In addition to her own home, Miss Cherry also owned a two-bedroom cottage she rented to snowbirds for $1,500 a week. But she rented that cottage to me for the same $500 a month I had been paying for a room. And then she told me, "Don't worry about paying me anything right now. When you get a job, a paying job, let's sit down and we'll talk about it."

Living in the cottage was a much better situation. If I didn't have the money to pay her, I cleaned up her property, landscaped, did different little things like that around there. Miss Cherry blessed me. That's when I kind of lit up again.

Miss Cherry actually got me my first caregiving contract with a family that lived nearby, just a little walk around the corner. I cared for Charles Cleland, who had taught and coached at Sarasota High School for thirty-six years. He was well known in Sarasota, a local hero, and now he was elderly and had dementia. Every morning I would go there, get him up, clean him up, take him to appointments, and get him down at night. I cared for him until he died.

Other people in the church found out I did that. I took care of the dads of a couple other families from Bayside. God was opening doors. Not only opening doors, but using me. One man I took care of, Bill Gordon—I ministered to him and his wife, and led him to the Lord when he was in his nineties. Later, after he died, his wife called to tell me she was saved too.

Meanwhile my volunteer ministering at Sarasota County Jail was growing. The chaplain at the jail in Port Charlotte, about an hour away, heard about what I was doing and asked me to volunteer there. Later, when he left, the Port Charlotte jail hired me as a full-time chaplain.

Of course, at that time I had no idea of all that God had planned for me in Florida.

16

What God
Purposed To Be

Bayside Community Church has a growth track, a series of sessions introducing folks to how the church is set up, how to discover their purpose, and build their faith. At the time, one step of this track was a twelve-week small group called CORE. In 2013 I started teaching CORE as a volunteer. I was serving in this, my first role with Bayside, when I met Stephanie, the woman who is now my wife.

My Marriage

I was coming into the church one fall day in 2013, after I had been outside greeting. I was walking through the foyer, heading toward the sanctuary, and I walked past a striking brunette with intelligent, intense hazel eyes. I felt a leap in my spirit.

I immediately stopped and went back, and said, "Do I know you?"

She smiled and said, "No, but I know you." Her voice was pleasant, deep and strong.

My head jerked back a touch and I said, "Really!" I was smiling right back.

Stephanie said she had seen Pastor Craig point me out and announce what I was doing in the prison ministry. She wanted to talk to me about it because she felt that prison ministry and mission work was a good mix, one she thought her adopted Haitian son would be interested in.

I said to her, "Well, we need to get together to talk." I started doing the pastor thing, telling her about the growth track. I asked her what she was doing the next week and I said, "Why don't you join us in CORE? I'm one of the teachers there."

She said, "Okay, I'll do that."

Stephanie came the next week but I wasn't there; I ended up working at the Port Charlotte jail that day. She still tells people that "he invited me to CORE and he wasn't even there!"

The week after that I saw Stephanie again at church. I said, "So what's up?"

She gave me a look. "I came to class and you weren't there."

I said, "Yeah, I'm a chaplain and I teach at the Charlotte County Correctional Facility. I had to be there early last week, so I couldn't make it to CORE. But let's exchange email addresses because I really want to talk to you."

We set up to have dinner at a restaurant in Sarasota. When we met there I started out asking her questions about her personal relationship with God, but then my questions started getting a lot more personal. About halfway through dinner Stephanie said, "Wait a minute. Is this a date?"

I grinned, "Pretty much."

She had been under the impression our getting together was about prison ministry. But actually, the day I had first met Stephanie, I left the church and went to teach at the jail. That day I told the guys there, "I met my wife today; she just doesn't know it yet."

We got married May 24, 2014.

~~~~~~

Stephanie's Story

I had been single for about six or seven years when we met. I had been going to Bayside's East Bradenton Campus with Emerson, my only son left at home. When the East Sarasota campus opened up we visited one time, thinking that since we're Sarasota people and my son goes to school in Sarasota that might be the place to go. It didn't feel comfortable, so we went back to the East Bradenton Campus.

We tried East Sarasota Campus again but just kind of looked at each other, and said, "Ehhh, I don't know."

That summer of 2013 I was at a place in my life that I had done the faith step and given everything back over to God. Up to then I had been trying to repair myself, and I had been thinking

I had God on my side; but I still was running the show, trying to do it all my way. So that big faith step was about letting Him do it His way. Letting Him do it His way meant hands off for me, and just serving Him, being ready for Him. I knew I needed to be back into serving others. I needed to be serving where God wanted me to serve. So I asked Him where that was.

I thought I needed to be back in youth ministry. At my previous church I had been an assistant to the high school youth pastor for almost nine years. It had felt good; I enjoyed it, but when I tried to get into that ministry again it didn't feel comfortable.

One Sunday morning I realized, "I'm trying to push the buttons again." God literally made it clear to me that I needed to go to the East Sarasota Campus and stay.

I told my son, "We are going to the East Sarasota Campus today and we're going to stay. This is going to be our campus from now on."

Why?" he asked.

I said, "God told me that everything that I need to be doing for Him is there. And I don't know what that is, but He told me to stay there and then it's going to happen."

We went and everything changed; it was so funny. My whole perspective changed. Instead of going to the church at a different campus and looking for things we didn't like so that we could compare, I went to that campus knowing that that's where God wanted me to be. That was the first time we met the campus pastor. Pastor Craig was right out front, saw us, and asked if this was our first time there. It wasn't, but I said yes. In a way, it was.

He saw Emerson, noticed his basketball shirt, and said, "There's another basketball player here; maybe you know him."

It ended up being one of Emerson's teammates and best friends from school. I was thinking, "Oh, this is all kinds of affirmation, God. You're really checking off all my boxes."

When I had been there for a couple of weeks I was still trying to figure out what God had planned for me. I heard about some Bayside programs and I was going to look into them and see if one of them would be a good place to serve.

One Sunday morning soon after, Pastor Craig announced he wanted us to stand up and pray for Irving Moody, who was doing jail ministry. I saw the man stand up in the front row and I immediately thought, "Well, I need to find out more about that. I'd really like to see whether God's calling me to that." It was the first time I had noticed him. Something stirred in me. It didn't scare me, but I knew that something stirred in me.

I attempted to try to talk to him after church, and it didn't work. For the next two or three weeks, it was the same thing: I would see him in church, but after church he either was gone too fast or there were too many people around him. I just didn't push.

By that point I had just kind of given up, saying, "Well, Lord, I guess You're going to have to do something a little bit stronger, because whatever that feeling was, I can't even get to talk to this man." Until one day . . .

As I was getting ready to go into the sanctuary he walked right past me. He turned around, looked at me and said, "Do I know you?"

I said, "No, but I know you."

He looked surprised and asked me why. I told him I'd wanted to talk to him about the jail ministry since the morning we had been asked to pray for him."

He said, "Oh. Well, we need to talk."

After he invited me to the CORE class and then was not there at it, I did not know what to make of this guy. When I next saw him and he said we need to talk, I said okay, thinking, "Yeah, we do, because I'm still interested in this jail ministry and I've got this guy in front of me now and I'm going to get some information."

He said, "Here's my email. Email me." I thought that was funny, but now I don't because I'm his wife and he has me do everything for him that way. He's not a detail person. He said, "Email me so we can figure something out."

So I emailed him that week and he set up a time for Friday night. We met at a restaurant and he started asking me all these questions about my walk with God. I was trying to get in a couple questions about the jail ministry, but he seemed to be leading the conversation and gradually . . . the questions changed.

He asked about my adoption of Emerson from Haiti, and he was really intrigued by that, so I told him all the ups and downs. I felt really comfortable, and I was thinking, "He knows I'm single," so I talked a lot about my divorce.

Then the questions started to get real personal. Things like, "What's your birthday?" And, "What do you like? What do you like to do for fun?" Nothing that had anything to do with jail ministry.

I stopped. Something clicked in my head. I literally leaned forward, grabbed his arm, leaned into him and said, "Wait a minute. Is this a date?"

His words were exactly, "Pretty much."

And I said, "Oh."

That just told me right off how important it was to him that I was a woman that sought God, not religion, and that was the whole reason for the interview. It had nothing to do with the jail ministry. He wanted to know (and it wasn't until later that I found this out) if what he had felt that first day we met was from God.

Later, after we had dated for a couple months, he told me that he had gone to the jail that very day we met and told the inmates, "I met my wife today; she just doesn't know it yet."

I really kind of blew that off, thinking, "That's just guy talk," because I kept asking, "How would you know that after just a few words? You didn't know if I was a maniac, you didn't know if I like to sleep all day and not at night, you didn't know if I was ever going to cook for you—you didn't know anything about my personality."

I thought that way until the first day I went into the jail. That was in February after we were engaged. As I walked down the hall, a trustee mopping the floor looked up and said, "You must be Mrs. Moody." He told me what Irving had said that first day, which blew my mind.

It was really kind of cool because by that point I knew my soon-to-be husband's heart. He had heard from God the day we'd met, and later as part of our courting he told me God confirmed I was the one because of what Irving had asked God for: that he and his wife would go into the jail and he would go one way, into the men's pod, and his wife would go another, into the women's pod.

So I knew what I was walking into as a commitment to him and there was never a place in my spirit where I questioned that. I knew that he was seeking a wife, and he was telling God, "You already know what my heart's desire is, God, so you just need to let me know when it's the right one." That's why he had that feeling when we met.

And for me, it was almost the same way. I wanted to be married again, but I figured, if I really have faith in God, I'll just put it out of my mind. I knew God was telling me I needed to serve Him while I was my repairing myself. I told God, "I'm going to serve you and you've got to take care of the rest."

I knew God was preparing a husband for me, because I had asked Him to. I asked Him for a man of God, a godly man. I didn't realize He was going give me a man who ran after God like Irving does. I think God performed above and beyond, like He always does. So really, both of us in our own way trusted God for a mate.

That's why it was so easy for me to walk into our marriage. Our first date was October 16, 2013. We were engaged on December 21. That's when I got the ring, but we knew weeks before that we were going to get engaged.

There were a number of people who asked, "How long have you known each other? Or, "How long have you been dating?" I quickly realized my answer was, "Exactly the right amount of time."

When God puts everything in place why would I question what He has done? When two become one that's a God thing. It's not something that happens overnight; it's not any easier when you get older and wiser and think you know better. You are still going to have those rough edges of learning how to become one.

We're thankful that we have God because there's no way you can become one unless you have that third party involved, God.

On Staff at Bayside

Even though I had already been an ordained pastor in Georgia and Virginia, and a chaplain, I went through Bayside's entire leadership track, and in May 2015 I was ordained as a pastor through Bayside. That same year, as the church leadership saw me continuing to make disciples as a volunteer teaching CORE, Bayside hired me as Director of Discipleship.

Ever since my time with Kenny, through my times of questioning and discouragement, God was telling me, "Just don't faint. Don't give up. Keep your eyes on me. Trust in me. Everything that you're going through is for your good. It's working stuff out of you that I can't use, that you can't bring into my presence."

My Son

I now have a good relationship with my son. In 2013 we connected and I was able to tell him how sorry I was that I wasn't there for him as he grew up. I talk with my son at least twice a month. He and his girlfriend, Andrea, have a son, Rashaud Jr.

The three of them visited Stephanie and me in 2016. During that visit God orchestrated healing between us like only He can. Rashaud's son acted out a bit and I stepped in with the grandpa thing and spoke to Little Rashaud. As I did, my son went into the garage, so I followed him. I said, "Look, Man, this is the deal; you need to be able to speak into his life. When Little Rashaud acts out like that, he's asking for your attention, and your fiancée isn't always going to be there to deal with that. As a man you need to be able to step up and tell him what's right or wrong. He should know it just by the look on your face; you shouldn't even have to say anything."

He said, "Pop, I know. Sometimes I just don't feel like I know what I'm doing. I don't feel like I know what to say." Rashaud broke into tears. "Man, I just don't know what to do. Every time I try to do what's right I always screw it up."

I held my son, and cried with him. I pressed his head to my shoulder, and said, "C'mere, Man, let me tell you something about you. See, you are my seed. If we are nothing else, we are survivors. We have survived a lot of stuff, Rashaud. And the same thing that is in me is in you."

I told him, "You can be whatever you want to be, Rashaud. I believe in you." The same words my dad had told me.

At that time Rashaud was not yet saved. So, I said, "You've just got to turn your life over to Christ and stop trying to do it yourself. That's what I had to do."

We stood there, my arms around him, crying together. So much needed to come out of him and so much I needed to speak into him. He said, "Pops, I never knew you were there; I never knew you loved me like this. I never knew you had my back." That statement hit me like a brick.

I told him, "I've never stopped loving you," because it really came down to him feeling not loved by me. I said, "You know I'm your dad. I'll always be your dad, and no matter what's going on in your life, you can always come to me and we can work things out."

Rashaud said, "I don't know how to be a man. I don't know how to lead. I look at you and you've got everything together." What he was looking at as being "together" was that I was happily married and I had a house. He was looking at things.

This was my opportunity to share with him, "Success is not about things; it's not just about what you've got because, yeah, I've got a place and I've got a wife and we're doing good, but that's not what makes me who I am. Real success is through Christ, our identity in Him. He has a purpose for my life and a purpose and plan for your life."

I wanted my son to understand that when I talk about what God purposed me to be I am telling about the fruit I am blessed with as a result of clinging to God on my journey. I realize that—like Job—I could lose it all, and it wouldn't destroy my faith in God and His plan for me. I would pick back up and follow where God leads.

Rashaud was able to *see* my life as I was being transformed. Seeing me changed moved him past any hurt he had from my not being there or the negative talk he had heard about me: "Your dad's no good, in and out of jail, a drug addict." Seeing me changed helped him forgive me for all those years of not being there for him. I couldn't just tell him how I was changed; that kind of stuff had to be walked out. He had to see it in me.

During that visit, Rashaud went into the jail with our ministry. I had always been talking to my guys there about my son and how I had damaged that relationship and how God was putting it back together. So now, when he told the inmates how he felt growing up without a dad and how he then had been able to heal that hurt and now had a dad he could trust, a dad who loves him and is there for him, I'm telling you—there were many big, strong men crying in the room that day.

I am grateful to Rashaud's mom for the good job she did raising him without help from me. My son is actually in the process of changing his last name, changing it to Moody. I am so honored by that.

Healing Between People, Healing Between Races

After all these years I have a whole different attitude about people. I've learned to look for the good in people, and when I feel I'm taking offense I give the situation to God. Sometimes I still need to work things out between me and someone else or, as a pastor, between others; otherwise I can let it go, knowing God will deal with each of us.

About the race issue—well, I know some people are racist, sure. But some forces are at work in our country today drumming up a culture of rage and despair and ignoring the obvious truth that we have a multi-racial society.

Do I still look for instances of racism against me? No. I look for ways to heal it.

Jail Ministry Begins

In 2012, when I started volunteering at the Sarasota County Jail, I was laying the groundwork for teaching in the jail. Back then there were no faith-based cellblocks, or what we call God Pods. Sarasota jail holds about 1,500 male and female inmates; once a week inmates from different floors could sign up for Christian service in their sixty-seat chapel. Besides me, people from other organizations like the Salvation Army, NA, AA, and a parenting group rotated in to speak.

When I started maybe fifteen guys would come to chapel. I offered to take every slot I could to speak the message to the men.

God put details in place like only He can. Since I was there during the day when other volunteers were working their regular jobs, I began to get very connected to the jail captains, sergeants and lieutenants because they saw me frequently, going in to preach or being called in to do death notifications.

The chapel started filling up because guys were going back to their pod, saying, "Man, they've got a brother that's bringing the Word." Now there were forty-five or fifty guys that wanted to go to chapel. It just blew up. That's when I started the paid chaplain position at Port Charlotte Jail, which also housed both men and women.

Through Bayside I got a small co-ed group started for volunteers to go into the jail. I required the group to go through Bayside's growth track so they would be trained for leadership. It was around this time that Stephanie and I met. When she joined the jail ministry small group I felt so humbled and grateful that God had answered my prayer about my wife.

The success of the Sarasota chapel services opened up the door for me to sit down with the jail administrators and talk with them about having people from different units in the jail volunteer to live in a faith-based pod. The major at the jail then wasn't a faith-based person, but his replacement was. It didn't happen overnight, but because the pod where all the trustees were housed needed some work, they moved the trustees; and where they moved them ended up being a better permanent trustee spot. And that left a fifty-bed pod available; that became our faith-based pod. It started with men only, as a pilot. But my vision was for women to get the same thing.

All this happened so when the jail administrators said to me, "Pastor, are you still trying to get your faith-based pilot program in here? How many leaders to you have?" I was able to say, "We have a team of six men and six women trained and ready to go."

By 2018 the jail ministry was in four jails in this area as well as a prison, Hardee County Correctional Facility. We grew to about forty volunteers, many serving as coaches to newer volunteers, working with over 1,000 inmates a year.

This program changes the lives of officers too, like the one who one day followed us outside the men's pod at Manatee Jail and said, "Pastor Moody, I just want to let you know I know Christ now because of what you've done in this pod."

To complement our faith teaching, Bayside volunteers Vivian Rowe and Mark Daniels wrote a Bible-based curriculum, "Road to Reentry," that teaches practical skills like how to write a resume and how to dress for an interview.

The real growth of our team came when we figured out how to download Bayside's weekly church service and take it in to the jail. We did that in Sarasota and when Manatee County Jail saw what was going on in Sarasota, they called and said we want to do that too. We began to train leaders from Bayside's other church campuses in the area.

It was spring of 2017 when I again found myself in a waiting time. I was volunteering, leading the growing jail ministry, while I was still doing my paid job, Director of Discipleship at Bayside's East Sarasota Campus. I was so busy, so stretched. During this time my boss at Bayside said to me, "Look, I know you're waiting here. We see your passion, we see your labor, we see what you're doing . . . give me a little bit of time." Once again I needed to tell myself, "I gotta believe, I believe God for this. I gotta believe they're just making the proper steps to transition."

And then I got called in and given the newly-created position of Pastor of Jail Ministries with an office at Bayside's main campus.

After doing the ministry through Bayside for a year I decided to continue the jail ministry apart from Bayside. I found more freedom to administer the program as God was leading me. This was a risky step of faith, one that meant once again abandoning security to trust in God for His provision.

You see, I want the inmates to know that where they are is a place not to give up hope; this is the place to look for your destiny, your redemption, your future. I tell them, "I did that. And let me show you how."

It all started with Romans 12:1-2. The whole jail and prison ministry is based on that Romans 12 text; and every leader, every volunteer in the ministry, is required to know that text by heart, be able to recite that text, and walk in it.

> I beseech you therefore, brethren, by the mercies of God, that you present your bodies a living sacrifice, holy, acceptable to God, which is your reasonable service. And be not conformed to this world: but be you transformed by the renewing of your mind, that you may prove what is that good, and acceptable, and perfect, will of God. (AKJV)

Being incarcerated is where many of us realized the call God had on our life. The guys that I see at the prison right now, they know their Word. They're in the Word. I mean they're around dope, but when I open that gate over in the jails, the inmates have got their Bibles in their hands, and they're waiting. They're hungry. They're being transformed.

We've had several guys volunteering and teaching in the jail ministry that once were in jail. They got out, got mentored for a year, and then they went back in—to teach. They can go in the jail and say, "I was in that bunk right there." That means a lot to the inmates because when they see someone who had been locked up for seven years or ten years who has turned his life around after getting out, it gives them hope. They think, "You did it; I can do it too."

I tell them all the time, "Walk it out; God's got a purpose and a plan for you."

Yes, I was transformed; but I am not a finished project. That is ongoing, ongoing still. Through all that, I made many mistakes, took detours, learned lessons, picked myself up and got going again. As an ex-con it took an extra dose of persistence to keep going. I urge you to read the Appendices in this book to get some keys to help you in your growth and transformation.

I am so grateful to Rev. Beard, to Kenny, and to the many others God used in my life. Their faith in God—and in me—started me on a path to life, not death.

Kenny spoke into my life; Rev. Beard helped me manifest Kenny's words spoken over me. It all started with Rev. Beard giving me that key and telling me to come in and clean up the church. I thank God for Rev. Beard's leadership. I really thank God for Rev. Beard's desire to walk with me and mentor me. He came alongside me and saw what I didn't see. He would tell me, "You got to put the work in because what God has purposed for you is way more than you can even expect right now."

So I pass on to you Rev. Beard's words, to remember whenever you face challenges: "Hang in there. Don't give up. Put in the work now, remembering what God has purposed to be for YOU is way more than you can even expect."

Don't worry or think God doesn't care about you. And don't worry or think that you've done something so bad God won't forgive you, or that you are in such a bad place He won't want you.

He'll meet you wherever you are.

APPENDICES

Your Invitation

If you do not yet have a personal relationship with Jesus, I invite you to pray this now:

Dear God,

I realize that we can't earn salvation; we are saved by your grace when we have faith in your Son, Jesus Christ. I realize all I have to do is believe I am a sinner and that Christ died for my sins, and ask for His forgiveness.

Then, my next step is to turn from my sins; I know this to be repentance. Jesus Christ knows me and loves me. Lord, I realize that what matters to You is my honesty and the attitude of my heart.

Dear God, I ask for Your forgiveness. I believe Jesus Christ is Your son. I believe Jesus died for my sin and that You raised Him to life. I agree to trust Him as my Savior and follow Him as Lord from this day forward. Guide my life and help me to do Your will. I pray this in the name of Jesus. Amen.

Congratulations! If you have prayed this prayer, you have received Christ as your Savior and have made the best decision you will ever make, one that will change your life forever! I encourage you to get connected with a church or faith group of like-minded Christians and enjoy the support you'll get there. I also suggest you talk to your church about water baptism.

Keys to Transforming Your Life

No matter what kind of growth or change you want to make for your life, here are important keys. This is not meant to be the complete summary of what it will take you—you can find lots of books on that subject. But this will get you started.

Be in the Word/Choose a Life Verse/Learn Power Verses

All Scripture is breathed out by God and profitable for teaching, for reproof, for correction, and for training in righteousness, that the man of God may be complete, equipped for every good work.

—2 Timothy 3:16-17 (ESV)

Start your day reading the Bible. You'll find God's Word the best guide for your life.

When you grow in your relationship with Christ the Holy Spirit gives you life verses. Life verses and power verses are similar; power verses are the Bible verses that strongly speak to you and that apply to what God is calling you to. Your life verse is the one that speaks to you most deeply spiritually. You may have more than one life verse, especially as you grow. Romans 12:1-2 is one of my life verses. Write your verses on sticky notes and place them on your mirror and around your house, car, and workplace.

Commit verses to memory. King David sang the praises of knowing God's Word. He said, "I have hidden your word in my heart that I might not sin against you" (Psalm 119:11).

Pray

> *And pray in the Spirit on all occasions*
> *with all kinds of prayers and requests.*
>
> *—Ephesians 6:18*

If you're not used to praying you may worry you won't do it "right." Please let that go. Just talk to God and listen for answers.

Jesus gave us a simple prayer. When his disciples asked Him to teach them how to pray, Jesus "said to them, 'When you pray, say: Father, hallowed be Your name. Your kingdom come. Give us each day our daily bread. And forgive us our sins, for we ourselves also forgive everyone who is indebted to us. And lead us not into temptation'"(Luke 11:2-4 NASB).

Set aside time daily to relate with God (talking *and* listening) like you would with any other special relationship. You can find articles online and books on prayer; also learn from others who pray.

Commit to the Truth

> *Do not lie to one another, seeing that you*
> *have put off the old self with its practices.*
>
> *—Colossians 3:9 (ESV)*

No excuses. Covering up the truth won't make you look good. Being strong and telling the truth does.

Find a Group/Join a Group /Get Support

> *Not neglecting to meet together, as is the habit*
> *of some, but encouraging one another.*
>
> —*Hebrews 10:25 (ESV)*

Celebrate Recovery, Life Recovery, AA, NA, small groups at your church—or another church—all are available to you. Go. Find one that works for you. Stay.

Get an Accountability Partner

> *Iron sharpens iron, and one man sharpens another.*
>
> —*Proverbs 27:17 (ESV)*

At the beginning of every one of my semesters in prison ministry, when I go before the inmates, I say, "One of the most important things you can do when you get out of this jail is get an accountability partner."

What that means is get in a space with another person that's doing the right thing that you tell the truth to, that you can be open and transparent with, and go through the hard stuff with. It's not for him or her to judge you; it's for him or her to hold you accountable.

I think every person in this world needs another person to be accountable to. Inmates that get out of jail in our area can find one very easily, because we've got support groups already set up for them.

Inmates who get out in other parts of the state or the country can find the nearest church that has Celebrate Recovery, or Life Recovery, and find an accountability partner. And that accountability partner may be a pastor.

There's a lot of overlap between mentor and accountability partner, but the difference is an accountability partner is usually someone on the same point in the path as you. A mentor is someone further along the path, who can share his or her experience with you.

An accountability partner holds you accountable for the things that you say you're doing, or the things that you should be doing.

Let's say I've told my accountability partner that when I get upset during a conversation with my wife I'm not going to just shut down the conversation, but I will come back and we'll talk and resolve the issue. And my accountability partner says, "Did you go back and resolve the issue with your wife this week?" That's accountability.

Get a Mentor

And let us consider how to stir up one another to love and good works.

—*Hebrews 10:24 (ESV)*

I started out meeting with Rev. Beard in Charlottesville and he spoke into my life a whole transformative way of living. When I came to Sarasota, Florida, I submitted to

Pastor King. We started out meeting every week, then every two weeks for about three years. We still meet. Through the years I also have continued to be mentored by Pastor Beard.

We can all use a mentor. We all need to have our life spoken into. Generally, mentors don't find you. You find one and initiate the relationship.

You may find a mentor through a group like Celebrate Recovery, NA or AA.

Have a Vision for your Life

> *Write the vision, and make it plain.*
>
> —*Habakkuk 2:2 (AKJV)*

and

> *They devoted themselves to the apostles' teaching and to fellowship, to the breaking of bread and to prayer.*
>
> —*Acts 2:42*

Even before I had a family, even before I met my wife, I carried a statement with me that I wrote when I was in prison. I titled it "The Moody Family Vision Statement."

A part of the vision statement, inspired by Acts 2:42, reads: "The members of this family, having been brought together by God for this time to work in and take care of our ministry, will devote themselves to the reading, study, teaching and practice of the Word, fellowship among themselves and other family members, the breaking of bread, and prayer." That vision statement is now reproduced on a big canvas on my wall.

On a shelf in my living room is a model of the Eiffel Tower. On another wall is a photograph of it, and on still another wall is a stylish rendering of the tower, done in white on black. Paris. That's our dream vacation.

What are your dreams? Get them clear. They're from God; submit them to Him, and keep them alive with positive, vivid reminders of them—a vision statement, pictures, models, sayings, sticky notes on your mirror.

One important benefit of having a clear vision—and your goals are part of that vision—is when you are discouraged or face setbacks, your vision will encourage you to persist.

Disciple Others

Therefore go and make disciples of all nations.

—Matthew 28:19

As a prison ministry pastor I try to prepare for that time when the inmates come out, to get them plugged into the body of Christ. Plugging into the body of Christ means joining support groups, coming to church, doing Bible studies. As people who are being discipled, they understand the Scripture that tells them now you go and make disciples of all men.

Pastor Craig King teaches that if you keep taking in education but not pouring it out you'll be like a stopped-up pond, stagnant. But if you pour out to others you'll be like a flowing river, clean, fresh and healthy.

As you grow, you will find yourself in a position to influence others, to help them grow spiritually. Coming alongside others individually or in a group and pouring into them spiritually is discipling them. However, keep in mind it is the Holy Spirit in us that causes spiritual growth. Our role is to obey what Holy Spirit is telling us, like when we pray and we hear or feel God telling us to do this, go there, talk to that person.

Mentoring and discipleship are similar but discipleship focuses on spiritual growth, while mentoring may focus on specific areas apart from or including spiritual growth. Rev. Beard both mentored and discipled me.

Successful Relationships

Finishing is better than starting. Patience is better than pride. Don't be quick-tempered, for anger is the friend of fools.

—*Ecclesiastes 7:8-9 (NLT)*

Part of loving the Lord is to seek first the kingdom of God in all that we do, including all our relationships. As an example, look at my marriage. How is my marriage with Stephanie different from the way I viewed relationships before Rev. Beard? One way is accountability. Stephanie and I have agreed to meet with someone once a month, and be accountable in marriage. As I write this book we meet with another married couple.

I think every healthy, truly devoted Christ-following couple should have that in their marriage.

Now I do life with a Biblical worldview. And it's a big difference. Now I live a life that is not religious, but righteous; we are to live to be witnesses to others. There shouldn't be anything that I'm hiding, so I should be able to have an open and transparent place where I can invite people in.

Before I turned my life over to Christ I was like everyone else with a secular world view; I would never have brought anybody into my personal space with my wife because I was doing whatever the heck I wanted to do.

For example, in my previous relationships if we argued it often escalated into both of us cussing and yelling, and my leaving and drinking. It was out of control and it was damaging. In my marriage with Stephanie when I feel my anger rising I signal her and say something like, "I'm going to walk the dog." Then I go out for a walk . . . though I may not take the dog. She's not worried because she knows I'll be back and we'll talk. I cool off, we talk and we work it out. The more we do this the more our confidence grows that we will resolve our issues.

Power Verses for Victory

No weapon that is formed against you will prosper.

—Isaiah 54:17 (NASB)

He (the devil) is a liar and the father of lies.

—John 8:44

Greater is He who is in you than he who is in the world.

—1 John 4:4 (NASB)

*In all these things we are more than conquerors
through him who loved us.*

—Romans 8:37

If God is for us who can be against us?

—Romans 8:31

*Trust in the Lord with all your heart
And do not lean on your own understanding.
In all your ways acknowledge Him,
And He will make your paths straight.*

—Proverbs 3:5-6 (NASB)

*If anyone is in Christ, he is a new creature; the old things
passed away; behold, new things have come.*

—2 Corinthians 5:17 (NASB)

*Write this to Philadelphia, to the Angel of the church. The
Holy, the True—David's key in his hand, opening doors no
one can lock, locking doors no one can open—speaks: 'I see
what you've done. Now see what I've done. I've opened a
door before you that no one can slam shut. You don't have
much strength, I know that; you used what you had to keep
my Word. You didn't deny me when times were rough.'*

—Revelation 3:7-8 (MSG)

*Now I want you to know, brothers and sisters,
that what has happened to me has actually
served to advance the gospel.*

—Philippians 1:12

*I will praise you to all my brothers;
I will stand up before the congregation and testify
of the wonderful things you have done.*

—Psalm 22:22 (TLB)

*The faithful love of the Lord never ends!
His mercies never cease. Great is his faithfulness;
his mercies begin afresh each morning.*

—Lamentations 3:22-23 (NLT)

*God is faithful; he will not let you be tempted
beyond what you can bear. But when you are tempted,
he will also provide a way out so that you can endure it.*

—*1 Corinthians 10:13*

*These trials will show that your faith is genuine. It is
being tested as fire tests and purifies gold—though your
faith is far more precious than mere gold. So when your
faith remains strong through many trials, it will bring
you much praise and glory and honor on the day when
Jesus Christ is revealed to the whole world.*

—*1 Peter 1:7 (NLT)*

*I do not understand what I do. For what I want to do I do
not do, but what I hate I do. And if I do what I do not
want to do, I agree that the law is good. As it is, it is no
longer I myself who do it, but it is sin living in me. For I
know that good itself does not dwell in me, that is, in my
sinful nature. For I have the desire to do what is good,
but I cannot carry it out. For I do not do the good I want
to do, but the evil I do not want to do—this I keep on
doing. Now if I do what I do not want to do, it is no
longer I who do it, but it is sin living in me that does it.*

—*Romans 7:15-20*

History of First Baptist Church on West Main Street, Charlottesville, Virginia

This church has an amazing history:

- First Baptist Church of Charlottesville was originally founded in August 1831 as Charlottesville Baptist Church.[1]

- Before the Civil War this was Charlottesville's only church that brought all races together to worship—but in separate, segregated areas. African-American Baptists attended service in the balcony only.[2]

- In 1863 about 800 African-Americans applied to start their own church so they could worship on the main floor and be part of church decisions.[2]

- After they got approval, the new congregation met in the basement of the same church building until 1868.[3]

- As Virginia law then required, the African-American church had a white pastor, Reverend John Randolph, to oversee the church and take tithes.[4]

- Their third and last white pastor, the Reverend John Walker George, helped the black church group move to the basement of what was originally a hotel built in 1828, and form Delevan Baptist Church in 1868.[2]

- Accounts differ: Some say that in 1870 the church hired their first black minister.[4] Another account says former slave William Gibbons became the church's acting preacher by the spring of 1866. [5]

- In 1876 the old building was torn down and the church members themselves began construction on the same site.[2]

- To avoid taking out a loan for the building the African-American church members built the building themselves, working on it after their regular work, often by lantern. Entire families helped: the women served food and the children carried bricks to the men.[3]

- Construction was completed on October 12, 1883; the church was dedicated on January 2, 1884; and was renamed on February 17, 1884, as the First Colored Baptist Church of Charlottesville.[3, 6]

- According to history about Thomas Jefferson's Monticello, after the Civil War one of the first activities of newly freed slaves was founding churches, and many freed slaves became ministers.[7]

Resources:

[1] https://www.fbcparkstreet.com/welcome-to-our-church/im-new/history/

2. http://www.aahistoricsitesva.org/items/show/138?tour=11&index=11

3. http://westmaincorridor.blogspot.com/2010/04/first-baptist-church.html

4. https://www.hallowedground.org/African-American-Heritage/First-Baptist-Church-Charlottesville

5. http://www.latinamericanstudies.org/slavery/Gibbons_William.pdf

6. http://www.cvillepedia.org/mediawiki/index.php/First_Baptist_Church_(West_Main_Street)

7. https://www.monticello.org/site/plantation-and-slavery/religion-vitality-spirit

I want to hear from you.
Contact me at irvingmoody1@gmail.com